Philosophy of the
Bhagavad Gita

ALSO AVAILABLE FROM BLOOMSBURY

An Introduction to Indian Philosophy, by Christopher Bartley

Divine Self, Human Self, by Chakravarthi Ram-Prasad

Doing Philosophy Comparatively, by Tim Connolly

The Bloomsbury Research Handbook of Indian Aesthetics and Philosophy of Art, edited by Arindam Chakrabarti

The Bloomsbury Research Handbook of Indian Ethics, edited by Shyam Ranganathan

Understanding Asian Philosophy: Ethics in the Analects, Zhuangzi, Dhammapada and the Bhagavad Gita, by Alexus McLeod

Philosophy of the *Bhagavad Gita*

A Contemporary Introduction

KEYA MAITRA

BLOOMSBURY ACADEMIC
LONDON · NEW YORK · OXFORD · NEW DELHI · SYDNEY

BLOOMSBURY ACADEMIC
Bloomsbury Publishing Plc
50 Bedford Square, London, WC1B 3DP, UK
1385 Broadway, New York, NY 10018, USA

BLOOMSBURY, BLOOMSBURY ACADEMIC and the Diana logo are trademarks
of Bloomsbury Publishing Plc

First published in Great Britain 2018
Reprinted 2019 (twice), 2020

A catalogue record for this book is available from the British Library.

Library of Congress Cataloging-in-Publicaton Data
Names: Maitra, Keya, author.
Title: Philosophy of the Bhagavad Gita : A Contemporary Introduction / Keya Maitra.
Description: London ; New York : Bloomsbury Academic, 2018. | Includes
bibliographical references and index. |
Identifiers: LCCN 2017039527 (print) | LCCN 2018005295 (ebook) |
ISBN 9781350040175 (ePub) | ISBN 9781350040168 (ePDF) |
ISBN 9781350040182 (paperback) | ISBN 9781350040199 (HPOD)
Subjects: LCSH: Bhagavadgâitâa–Criticism, interpretation, etc. | Hindu philosophy.
Classification: LCC BL1138.66 (ebook) | LCC BL1138.66.M346 2018 (print) |
DDC294.5/924046–dc23
LC record available at https://lccn.loc.gov/2017039527

ISBN: HB: 978-1-3500-4019-9
       PB: 978-1-3500-4018-2
       ePDF: 978-1-3500-4016-8
       eBook: 978-1-3500-4017-5

Typeset by Integra Software Services Pvt. Ltd.
Printed and bound in Great Britain

To find out more about our authors and books visit www.bloomsbury.com
and sign up for our newsletters.

To the memory of my mother
Maya Moitra
The first person in my life to teach me about the
depth, grandeur, and the certainty of the **Gita**

Contents

Acknowledgments ix
How to Use This Book xi

Introduction 1

1 Arjuna's Sorrow 33

2 The Yoga of Knowledge (and Philosophy) 41

3 The Yoga of Action 53

4 The Yoga of Renunciation of Action through Knowledge 61

5 The Yoga of Renunciation 69

6 The Yoga of Meditation 75

7 The Yoga of Knowledge and Judgment 83

8 The Yoga of the Imperishable *Brahman* 89

9 The Yoga of Sovereign Science and Sovereign Secret 95

10 The Yoga of Divine Manifestations 101

11 The Yoga of the Vision of the Cosmic Form 107

12 The Yoga of Devotion 117

13 The Yoga of Difference between the Field and the Field-Knower 123

14 The Yoga of the Division of Three *Gunas* 131

15 The Yoga of the Supreme Purusha 139

16 The Yoga of the Division between the Divine and the
       Demonic 145

17 The Yoga of the Threefold Faith 151

18 The Yoga of Liberation and Renunciation 157

Selective Glossary of Sanskrit Terms 169
References 171
Index 174

Acknowledgments

As this book goes into production I hope it will be helpful to inspiring students of the *Gita*. But I am also mindful of Krishna's counsel that one has claim over one's actions alone and never over the fruits of actions, and therefore, one must not live for the fruits of action. However, without the generous support of many friends, colleagues, and students, this fruit of my labor would have been substantially inferior. I have worked on this project for nearly ten years. This Acknowledgments would be too long if I tried to name all from whom this project has profited during this long interval. But any merit of this book would not be possible without the critical and insightful comments, suggestions, and encouragements of the following individuals: Heather Hardy for inspiring and challenging me to imagine what this project could be; Daniel Kolak for initially encouraging me to commence on this project; Simon Brodbeck for his extensive comments on an earlier draft that also helped me envision the Philosopher's Corners; Stephen Phillips for his generous sharing of his extensive knowledge of the *Gita* and constant encouragement; Catherine Parker for her thoughtful, yet astute, comments on multiple previous drafts; Colleen Coalter, my editor at Bloomsbury, for her brilliant guidance; Elizabeth Schiltz, Laura Guerrero, Jeremy E. Henkel, Emily McRae, Kisor Kumar Chakrabarti, and Jay L. Garfield for their deep philosophical sensibility, and dedication to authenticity, clarity, and rigor; Kelly Sloan, Merritt Moseley, Jill Yarnall, Amy Hannon, and Katherine Zubko for their generosity with their time, and careful comments on various previous drafts. I also want to share my deep sense of gratitude to my current and former students: Carson Nickels, John Fate Faherty, Matthew McIlhenny, and numerous students in my Asian Philosophy course over the years for their enthusiasm for this project and their specific help in the preparation of this translation. Finally, members of my family, especially Mohsin, whose love and sense of humor keep me grounded; my father and sisters who have been tremendous with their love and constant moral support; and my son Abir, whose very being continues to teach me an expansive sense of life. I dedicate this work to the memory of my mother who surely would have been the happiest to see this project coming to fruition.

Keya Maitra
Asheville, North Carolina

How to Use This Book

Taking my experience of teaching the *Gita* at two undergraduate institutions in the United States over the past decade into account, this book tries to attain the happy medium between readability and accuracy as well as provide a solid sense of the philosophical concepts on which the themes and ideas of the *Gita* stand. Different translators of the *Gita* into English have wavered between rendering the Sanskrit terms denoting main concepts into English and leaving them in Sanskrit. While the first approach provides easy accessibility, the latter approach tries to capture the internal and contextual complexity of many of these concepts. Further, as R. C. Zaehner writes, "many of the keywords of the Gita are so ambivalent in meaning as to make such an 'accurate' [single English] translation impossible without either misrepresenting the original or failing to bring out the multiplicity of meaning these keywords contain in any single instance" (1969, 4). Since many of these concepts, for example, *yoga, dharma*, and *guna*, are used in the *Gita* with a range of meanings in different contexts, I have decided to follow the latter approach. Further, since a particular meaning in which such a term is used in a context is not always clear, I believe leaving the term in Sanskrit allows the reader to determine the meaning for herself using the Glossary that I have provided following the translation, which is intended to supplement the translation. Whenever a term is left in Sanskrit and is italicized in the translation, it denotes one such concept. I have also left some other terms in Sanskrit (e.g., "Prakriti," "Purusha") not because they necessarily denote a multitude of meanings, but because the common English words that are used as their translation ("Nature" in the case of "Prakriti" or "Spirit" in the case of "Purusha," for example) fail to capture their meanings in the context of the *Gita*.

However, a major conceptual term that I have translated is "karma" partly due to its wide use in the popular culture of the West. One might even have seen the bumper sticker "My Karma ran over your Dogma." However, from the perspective of Hinduism and the *Gita*, the idea of karma has very little to do with the idea of dogma. So to minimize misreading, I have rendered the term "karma" as "action" in the present translation. I have also followed the convention of translating every epithet used for Krishna and Arjuna. For each epithet, I provide the name of the person referred to by that epithet when it is used for the first time in a chapter. Subsequently, I allow each epithet to stand on its own when it is repeated in the same chapter. However, given that Arjuna only addresses Krishna in the course of the *Gita*, all of the epithets he uses address Krishna. Therefore, I decided not to specify Krishna as the bearer of those epithets in the text.

My aim in the following Introduction is to give an overview of the various contexts and philosophies of the *Gita*. Ultimately, I hope to show that the *Gita*'s unique importance is underlined by its adaptation of disparate philosophical and religious themes of early South Asian religious thoughts into a cohesive, if not completely consistent, narrative. Let me also note here that in numerous classical translations of the *Gita* the translation is often accompanied by copious notes and commentaries. While they are invaluable for a Sanskritist, an Indologist, and a specialist in Indian philosophy, for most other readers they often present a halting access to the text. My hope is that by laying out the conceptual and philosophical groundworks in the Introduction, the translation will be able to stand on its own. Given my goal to enhance and facilitate Western readers' philosophical engagement with the *Gita*, however, I have appended each chapter with what I have called a *Philosopher's Corner: Chapter Analysis and Questions for Consideration*. There I draw attention to a few central issues with philosophical import that arise in the text, in addition to pointing out possible directions and questions for cross-cultural and comparative philosophical engagement.

Introduction

Let it be granted, that according to the letter of the
Gita it is possible to say that warfare is consistent with renunciation
of fruit. But after 40 years' unremitting
endeavour fully to enforce the teaching of the Gita in my own life,
I have, in all humility, felt that perfect
renunciation is impossible without perfect observance
of ahimsa [non-violence] in every shape and form.

—MAHATMA GANDHI,
THE COLLECTED WORKS OF MAHATMA GANDHI XLI, 100

R. C. Zaehner opens the Introduction to his well-regarded commentary and translation of the *Bhagavad Gita* (published in 1969) with the following question:

> During the last war we used to see notices everywhere asking if our journey [i.e. the resultant gas usage] was really necessary. In conscience we had often to admit that it was not. Today publishers might well ask authors: "is your *book* really necessary?" In the case of a new edition of the *Bhagavad-Gita* they would seem to be doubly justified in asking such a question. What, then, is the justification of the present work? (1969, 1)

Zaehner, of course, was referring to the numerous translations starting with the first English translation published by Charles

Wilkins in 1785 including the very popular ones of his time, by Edgerton (1944) and Radhakrishnan (1948). I believe that question is still very pertinent, if not more so, since there have been many more translations (and commentaries) published of the *Gita* (as the *Bhagavad Gita* is commonly referred to) between the time of Zaehner's Introduction and now. So what indeed is the justification of the present undertaking?

My response to this question will consist of two arguments. First, noting two prominent trends in almost all the English translations of the *Gita* used in a Western classroom, I will argue that the present translation aims at a middle point. The two trends are captured by the tendency either to tell the "pure" story of the *Gita* without considering its context, or to tell the "full" story of the *Gita* where every detail becomes necessary. These two trends emerge in response to two parallel challenges—both attempting to strike a balance—faced by any translation of the *Gita* intended mainly for a Western audience. The first challenge is to balance between the two goals of historical, textual, and religio-cultural accuracy on the one hand and accessibility and readability on the other that seem to pull in two opposite directions. Likewise, the second challenge is to balance between conveying the main message of the *Gita* clearly without getting lost in the background "noise" and providing an understanding of the cultural and especially philosophical underpinnings of the *Gita* that allow for a more nuanced capture of its multilayered and multifaceted message. What I have in mind especially in relation to this second balancing act is hinted at by Eric Sharpe, who argues that at least one of the predominant Western approaches to the *Gita* is to interpret it as "torn loose from its religious matrix" so much so that its being a Hindu scripture becomes "only incidental" (Sharpe 1985, xiii). In the same vein there are philosophers like Roy Perrett (1998) who attempt to understand the *Gita*'s ethical views and implications without considering them within the underlying Hindu systems of metaphysics.

I see these two trends exemplified in the existing academic translations of the *Gita*. While I cannot overstate my debt to Barbara Stoller Miller for a poetic rendition that makes the *Gita* very readable and ·accessible especially in a Western classroom, or to Zaehner whose translation is one of the most accurate and thorough, what I have missed is a translation that reaches a middle ground between the two. Since most audiences outside Southeast Asia do not grow up hearing the *Gita* recited at religious ceremonies or are familiar with the stories of the *Mahabharata* in which this text is situated, it might be tempting for the translator to try to tell the "pure" story of the *Gita* by extracting it from its religious and cultural heritage. I find this approach problematic because I don't think even the basic message of the *Gita* can be captured in its full complexity if pursued in terms of isolation. For example, many recent translations, including Miller's, omit the various epithets that Krishna, Arjuna, and Sanjaya use while addressing one another in the *Gita*. As a defense of this decision, Miller writes,

> The numerous epithets of Krishna and Arjuna, such as *Madhusudana*, "Slayer of Demon Madhu" for Krishna, or *Kaunteya*, "Son of Kunti" for Arjuna, have not been translated [in her 1986 translation]. Their meanings have resonance for an Indian audience, but for other readers they have little significance and are cumbersome in translation, so they have generally been normalized to the names Krishna and Arjuna. (1986, 17–18)

What this "normalization" fails to capture is the web of relationships which provides these characters history and context and finally meaning within the *Gita*'s relational worldview, namely, that individuals find meaning by discovering their location within the collective and not the other way around. The various epithets also "give us a sense of the flavor of that society the *Gita* was written about—archaic, heroic, and on the edge of its catastrophic doom" (Flood and Martin 2012, xxx).

The above discussion highlights the challenge and need to balance between contextualization and accessibility that I mentioned earlier. In this regard Gerald James Larson's insight is worth noting. He argues that the "deeper elegance and charm" of the *Gita* "are derivative of that transactional natural/cultural network which is India itself, and she [the *Gita*] cannot easily flourish elsewhere... [W]hen she is taken out of India to live permanently in a different medium—whether Latin or German or French or English—she becomes diminished" (Larson 1981, 514). Larson goes on to clarify that his argument is not against any translation of the *Gita*; rather, he questions whether the *Gita* "can live abroad permanently." Larson does not object to her travels so long as "she is introduced to strangers with tact and sensitivity" and so long as her "extended family"—the extended network of concepts and themes that form her context—are kept firmly in mind. The present translation has been mindful of Larson's insight.

Returning now to my second reason for this book, let me note that the *Gita* is often treated as mystical poetry (partly because its Sanskrit title literally stands for "*Song* of the Lord"); as such, the text does not require an understanding of its underlying philosophy in order to be appreciated. For example, in his 1968 translation Eliot Deutsch identifies remedying this mystical gloss as his motive, attempting to deliver a translation "designed specifically for Western students of philosophy and religion by a Western philosopher or teacher of philosophy" (Deutsch 1968, ix). My present endeavor could be viewed as extending Deutsch's specific project by not only providing the underlying Indian philosophical concepts, but also highlighting certain points of comparison between these and Western philosophical concepts. In this regard it is useful to add that interpreting the philosophical content of the *Gita*, even though not a widespread practice within the tradition of English translations of the *Gita*, has been a common feature of the traditional approach to this text in India starting with Sankara's *Gita-bhasya* in the eighth century. These Indian interpretations often treat the *Gita* as representative of a systematic development of a particular philosophical school and consequently present the *Gita* as a treatise in pure philosophy. Some non-Indian translators and commentators, Franklin Edgerton (1972) for example, diminish this approach by suggesting that whatever philosophy exists in the *Gita* is inconsistent or even incidental.

Part of the difficulty of translating the *Gita* for philosophy is because the nature and role of philosophy in the *Gita* are by no means clear or agreed upon. I agree with Madhav M. Deshpande's estimation in this regard when he writes,

His [Krishna's] exposition of philosophy is not an exercise in pure philosophy. It is applied philosophy, philosophy manipulated and reorganized to suit a special purpose. It is through this manipulation and reorganization of various strands that a new application of old philosophies is gradually developed and perfected. While the individual philosophical ideas in most cases are old, their peculiar redesigning and reorienting is the contribution of the author of the *Bhagavadgita*, or of Krishna himself as the Indian tradition believes. (1991, 346; see also Dasgupta 1975, 525)

So it seems to me that a "multitrack approach" that acknowledges the presence of multiple and diverse themes in the *Gita* is preferable to the "single-track approach" where the *Gita*'s metaphysics is considered as purely non-dualistic or purely theistic. However, even when an interpreter accepts that a synthesis of disparate themes—philosophical and socio-religious—happens in the *Gita*, one may characterize such synthesis differently. As Ramesh N. Patel clarifies, one might take a "syncretist approach" that treats the *Gita* as "combining mutually incompatible tracts" and as a result tries to find the "core" or the "original" *Gita* to which later layers get added over time (1991, 11). Or, one might take a "coherentist approach" which considers the *Gita* as offering "a more or less coherent integration" of different philosophical themes, spiritual paths, and their goals. Using this taxonomy of Patel, I could identify my approach as that of a multitrack coherentism. In fact, I believe that the internal diversity of the *Gita*'s message allows it to be relevant to a wide and diverse range of audiences—not just in terms of contemporary audience but also in terms of the *internal* audience of the *Mahabharata*. In addition to Arjuna, Sanjaya, and Dhritarashtra this internal audience includes those who are left in Hastinapur (capital of the Kurus), Janamejaya (a Kuru king considered to be the listener of the first narration of the *Mahabharata*) and his guests among others.[1]

Various contexts of the *Gita*

The *Gita and the evolution of Hinduism*

Writing on Hinduism in India and America, Larson comments, "If there is any one text that comes near to embodying the totality of what it is to be a Hindu, it would be the Bhagavad Gita" (Larson 2000, 132). Other scholars of the *Gita* (and Hinduism) have also noted its unique "pan-Hindu influence." What makes this unique is the fact that unlike Christianity and Islam there is no single holy text of Hinduism. The earliest set of texts of Hinduism which enjoys most authority is called the Vedas. Among the various themes and topics explored in the different sections of the four Vedas two divergent sets of questions seem most prominent. The first, rooted in the polytheistic tenets of Hinduism, asks, "what god shall we adore with our oblation?" (Ṛg Veda X.121, from Radhakrishnan and Moore 1957, 3). The second, however, is explicitly philosophical when it asks, "what is that which, being known, everything else becomes known?" (Muṇḍaka Upaniṣad I.i.3, from Radhakrishnan and Moore 1957, 38)

The main theme developed in response to the former set of questions is "a matter of commercial bargaining between the old, traditional gods and men. The gods control benefits, and grant them in exchange for the gratifications of the sacrifice" (Edgerton 1972, 179). As Ṛg Veda X.89.17 implores Indra, one of the principal gods, after offering praises and oblations, "O Indra, thus may we be made partakers of the new favours that shall bring us profit" (Griffith 1896, 469). The response to the second set of questions is marked by its reflective turn where hymns to gods and goddesses are replaced by a quest for fundamental answers regarding the ultimate nature underlying our everyday experiences of joys and sorrows, and myriad encounters of achievements and disappointments. They also explore the true nature of humanity and how that essence shapes the ultimate goal of a human life. The later Vedic texts of various Upanishads highlight the notion of *Brahman* understood as the ultimate reality that lies beyond the phenomenal world of birth and rebirth. It is the realization of one's true self to be *Brahman* thus achieving liberation from the cycle of rebirths that constitutes the ultimate goal of human life. As the Taittiriya Upanishad proclaims, "He who knows *Brahman* as the real, as knowledge, as the infinite, set down in the secret place [of the heart] and in the highest heaven, He obtains all desires, Together with the intelligent *Brahman*" (Radhakrishnan and Moore 1957, 59).

Against the backdrop of these two divergent themes—of pleading with the gods for rewards and boons versus self-realization—arose a special kind of people, the wanderers and spiritual seekers who rejected social order and conventions by leaving families, homes, and prescribed duties behind to pursue a way of becoming liberated from the suffering of the world. Such reorientations were attempted both inside and outside of the Hindu praxis. Thus, while the Upanishads were attempting to reform the ideals within the Vedic framework by their focus on renunciation as the ultimate goal of human life, Buddhism and Jainism were challenging some of the very basic core beliefs of the Vedic religion. As a result,

> There were new doctrines abroad that were being commonly accepted by the thoughtful. The doctrine of rebirth and particularly the dismal view taken of it were gaining wide currency and could not really be accommodated by the old [Brahmanical] system that saw in [prescribed] acts the cure of all afflictions. The cure *was* the affliction [for the reformists], for it was the acts themselves that were pointed to as the cause of endless reincarnation. (van Buitenen 1981, 13)

It is in this cultural backdrop of divergent themes that the crystallization of the core story of the epic *Mahabharata* occurs. In this context the *Mahabharata*—and especially the *Gita*—reshapes and reframes the Vedic themes by synthesizing early Vedic ritualism with the later Vedic introspective quest for liberation in a unique way. Instead of "external relinquishment, where one leaves home and social responsibility in favor of becoming a wandering mendicant" (Theodor 2010, 4–5), the *Gita* proposes "an internal relinquishment, by which one adheres to *dharma*, but makes an internal progress along the path of renunciation, by gradually learning to renounce the fruits of action, and then devote them to the supreme" (Theodor 2010, 5, italics in original). Krishna, is thus,

> made to reveal himself [in the *Gita*] as the guarantor of social stability, and the upholder of the *dharma* of class and life stage, who yet had the answer to the doctrine of rebirth that the heterodox [Buddhism and Jainism for example] had appropriated, who put their wisdom, philosophies, and renunciations in their place and who revealed himself as the savior of all. (van Buitenen 1981, 13)

This sentiment is echoed by Sharpe, who writes, "in an important sense Hinduism itself has been recreated on the Gita's foundations"

(Sharpe 1985, 175) and subsequently when Catherine A. Robinson writes, "the *Bhagavad Gita*'s rise to greatness is an important aspect of the reification of the Hindu tradition" (Robinson 2006, ix).

The Gita *within the* Mahabharata

Commenting on the *Gita*'s context, van Buitenen writes,

> The *Bhagavadgita* was conceived and created in the context of the *Mahabharata*. It was not an independent text that somehow wandered into the epic. On the contrary, it was conceived and developed to bring to a climax and solution the dharmic dilemma of a war which was both just and pernicious... [T]he *Gita* provides a unique religious and philosophical context in which it [the impending war] can be faced, recognized, and dealt with... [T]he *Gita* addresses itself in the first place to a specific issue that the Bharata war posed to a more reflective age, whose attitude toward violence was changing. (1981, 5–6)

The *Gita* is a part of the sixth book of the Indian epic *Mahabharata* that is believed to have been composed between 400 BCE and 400 CE, though the nucleus of the story of the epic was known much earlier. The *Mahabharata* is a story of a battle for control of the Ancient Northern Indian kingdom of Hastinapur. This battle took place between two sets of cousins of the same clan named Bharata. The main characters of the *Gita* are Arjuna (one of the main warriors involved in the battle) and Krishna (who is Arjuna's charioteer and, as becomes evident in the course of the *Gita*, a divine personification[2]). The *Gita* is an eighteen-chapter-long conversation between Arjuna and Krishna that ensues when seeing the two armies arrayed at the battleground with fighting about to begin Arjuna refuses to fight. What accentuates Arjuna's paralyzing moral dilemma is the interconnected narrative of the *Mahabharata*.

One of the opening events in the main narrative of the *Mahabharata* is the birth of Devavrata, the "grandsire," or the "grandfather" of the Bharata clan, who comes to be known as Bhishma because of his vow of celibacy. Due to complications relating to Bhishma's vow, the kingdom finds itself with two princes: the elder brother Dhritarashtra whose congenital blindness disqualifies him from the throne and younger brother Pandu who, though he becomes the king, remains unable to beget his own son due to a curse, and so renounces the throne and retires into the forest with his two wives. Dhritarashtra becomes the regent to the throne in the absence of an adult male heir. Meanwhile Dhritarashtra has a hundred sons and Pandu's two wives—Kunti and Madri—give birth to five sons with the help of five gods. After Pandu dies in the forest, Kunti brings the five young Pandava brothers to the court of Dhritarashtra. All the young princes—the sons of Dhritarashtra and the sons of Pandu, the Pandavas—are given all-round physical and moral training by their great-uncle Bhishma and priest Drona, a master of archery. As they grow up, the Pandava brothers surpass their cousins in every skill of martial arts and virtue, resulting in the jealousy of Dhritarashtra's eldest son Duryodhana.

In the next phase of the narrative, Duryodhana tries to deny the legitimate claim of Yudhishthira, the eldest Pandava, to the throne despite his being the oldest of all the cousins and being most qualified. After attempting to assassinate the Pandava brothers, Duryodhana manages to exile them for thirteen years. After returning from their exile, the Pandavas demand their share of the kingdom, but Duryodhana refuses. After several attempts to avoid war—including Krishna's trip to Duryodhana's court to plead for Yudhishthira's peace proposal—war seems inevitable as Duryodhana simply rejects any possibility of a compromise. Thus, even though the abomination of the war is unspeakable, it seems inevitable. As van Buitenen reasons, "while the Pandavas were clearly wronged, the only way to right the wrong is by committing the greater wrong of destroying the entire family" including the venerable elders who have joined the war on the Kaurava (i.e., Duryodhana's) side (1981, 2–3). That is the heart of Arjuna's dilemma. Further, the far larger size of the Kaurava army, clear to Arjuna from the assembled armies, gives rise to palpable doubt in his mind about the feasibility of a Pandava victory. What deepens the dilemma is the fact that this war is not simply a family feud but one with utmost moral consequence, not only because of the huge number of soldiers involved, but also because it is seen as a war between good and evil. However, this moral dimension does not follow from any necessary moral failure of family members on the Kaurava side. Rather, as Krishna reveals in the course of the *Gita*, this follows from how this war aligns with Krishna's grand plan. As he states in 4.7[3] and 4.8, whenever there is decline of righteousness, he assumes a human form "to protect the righteous and destroy the evil-doer" (4.8). In 11.33 Krishna makes the further claim that Arjuna's opponents in battle have already been killed by Krishna. From this perspective, it could be argued, as Patel does, that the *Gita* offers a just war philosophy (1991, 40). Even if that were the case, the metaphysical preoccupations of the *Gita* would make such a philosophy quite unlike any of the more familiar just war arguments in contemporary philosophy. In the latter case the focus is often on the rules and conventions of warfare and the nature of justification is articulated in human, rather than divine, terms.

Finally, a word on the character of Sanjaya in the *Gita*: as the armies of both sides stand arrayed ready for battle, Vyasa, the poet traditionally taken to be the author of the *Mahabharata*, appears before the blind king Dhritarashtra and grants him the chance of hearing an account of the battle as it takes place from Sanjaya, who is endowed with a "divine inner eye" that allows him to see all things past, present, and future. Sanjaya's report on the dialogue between Krishna and Arjuna thus assumes an error-proof authentic status given his direct access.

The conceptual underpinnings of the *Gita*

Rebirth and the law of karma

The *Gita*'s commitment to the concept of rebirth and use of it as a framework principle becomes evident early on when Krishna opens his rejoinder to Arjuna's decision to not fight as follows: "Just as the dweller of this body passes through childhood, youth and old age, so does it pass into another body" (2.13) and that "certain is birth for the dead" (2.27). Rebirth, simply speaking, stands for the Hindu belief that when one dies, there is an enduring, eternal part of one (which in the West is often called the soul but the *Gita* often refers to as the self) that endures and generally comes back to life in another physical form. Hindus believe in a cyclical, rather than linear, idea of time where no particular point in time is conceived as the start of time. Time is conceived as being without a beginning and in which various world cycles follow each other in an endless succession. A question following from this theory is how rebirth is determined; that is to say, when one is reborn, whether one should be born as a human or a lion or a toad or even as a divinity?

The response argues that the form of rebirth depends on one's karma. The law of karma is a universal moral law that maintains that every intentional action produces a residue (good or bad), implications of which have to be endured in the present life or in a later life, by the agent of that action. Stephen Phillips provides an account of the role of karma in one's rebirth and moral life when he writes,

> The most widely held picture is that an individual has both a sum of karmic worth and individual lines of karma that attract, like magnets, situations for discharge, karmic cathexis in worldly events causing pleasure and pain in various combinations and flavors. The aggregation depends on moral coefficients added to a total in the case of good karma and subtracted in the case of the bad, although the moral worth of some acts stands alone and invites reward or payback independently of the moral worth of the aggregate. The power of karmic vectors to affect events, especially outcomes of enterprises, is considered to be outside or beyond ordinary sensibilities, as is implied in the very word—unseen force, *adrishta*—used in all [Hindu philosophical] schools to refer to the causal power of karma's side of justice. (2009, 103)

While discussing the Hindu notion of the cycle of birth and rebirths (also referred to as *samsara*) it is also important to clarify how heaven and hell fit into this scheme. Unlike the Judeo-Christian context, where heaven and hell are treated as eternal destinations, the *Gita* conceives them within the cycle of rebirth. A substantial amount of good karmic residue will attain heaven for an individual. However, this is only a temporary station since when one exhausts that good karmic residue one must be reborn again. This is because liberation or freedom from *samsara*, not the attainment of heaven, is the ultimate goal of a Hindu[4] life. As the *Gita* clarifies:

> Men, knowers of the three Vedas, drinkers of the Soma, being purified of their sins, worship me with sacrifice seeking to win the way to heaven; attaining the holy world of Indra (king of the gods), they taste the divine delights of the gods in the celestial sphere. After enjoying the vast world of the heaven, they (re-) enter the mortal world when their merits have been exhausted; thus following the *dharmas* enjoined in the three Vedas, desiring desires, they attain what is transient. (9.20–21)

However, as Zaehner (1969, 24) worries, it remains unclear whether the *Gita* is consistent in maintaining that hell is a temporary station as well. Especially when one considers Krishna's following verse on the nature of a demonic person, it might be difficult to envision how such a self could attain a better station: "Falling into a demonic womb, deluded in birth after birth, they fail to ever attain me; O son of Kunti (Arjuna), they thus descend to the lowest depths" (16.20).

The Hindu system of class and caste

The diversity of one's next station, if one were to be reborn as a human, is captured in the concept of the Hindu system where different duties were prescribed for people belonging to different classes and stations (*varnashrama dharma*). While it is a matter of debate how this system came into practice, it is generally accepted that ancient Indian, namely, Aryan social life, gradually became hierarchical. There developed four main classes (*varna*), namely, Brahmin, Kshatriya, Vaisya, and Sudra. As Hutton writes, "The *varna* seem to have been originally the four classes into which Rigvedic society was divided; . . ., Brahman [Brahmin], Kshatriya and Vaishya, and fourthly the Sudra, below whom were the outcastes" (1969, 64). Their differences appear to fall along what their members do for a livelihood and what their respective duties are; the Brahmin or the priest caste has a duty to learn the Vedas, perform sacrificial rituals, and so on; the Kshatriya or the royal and warrior caste has a duty to rule the realm, lead and protect the people, and defend the above and one's honor by engaging in war when necessary; the Vaisya or the business caste has a duty to trade, farm, practice craftsmanship; and the Sudra or the servant caste has a primary duty to serve the other three castes in any way they demand. Sudras are also, in some contexts, taken to be the Outcaste (the lowest in the hierarchy considered "outside" of the caste system) whose main duties include carrying and cremating corpses, executing criminals, cleaning city and village streets and drains, and so on.

Another term that is often used in this context is "caste" which is used for the Hindi term *jati* or *jat* (Hutton 1969, 48). Even though the four classes mentioned above are at times referred to as castes (see, for example, Edgerton 1972, 161), as Hutton and others have argued, "caste" usually refers to smaller groups and subgroups that fall under these larger classes and are often governed by rules and conventions regarding intermarriage and ability to eat or drink together. This system of class and caste, as it was devised initially, was based on occupational skill or endeavor or one's aptitude. This theory is akin to Plato's *Republic* which divides society into four classes and argues "that a society as a whole functions best when each person in it knows his 'place' and works within it for his own self-fulfillment and for the good of all" (Deutsch 1968, 11). So a Brahmin would be one who is skilled at reciting chants and performing sacrificial rituals, a Kshatriya is one who is skilled at warfare. Because of this classification based on skill, at the time of the early Upanishads, there was also believed to be social mobility in the sense that one could be a Brahmin depending on what one's talents were irrespective of one's father's or mother's caste or class. However, by the time of the *Gita*, the castes came to be rigidly structured without allowing much room for social and economic mobility (see, for example, Aurobindo 1997, 512). If a child were born to a Sudra father, then irrespective of that child's talents and wishes, he would be a Sudra, and it would not be advisable for him to try to become a member of any other caste. As in the *Gita* Krishna advises, "Better to perform one's own duty even imperfectly than to perform another man's duties well; performing actions determined by one's own nature, a man contracts no sin" (18.47; see also 3.35). Since one's class and caste duties are determined according to one's nature (4.13), it seems that Krishna argues against social mobility.[5] In fact, the *Gita* provides one of the very first articulations of an argument for maintaining the stability of the social order against social mobility. In this regard Arjuna expresses a worry in the *Gita* about the ill effects that intermixture of class and castes create presumably by inter-caste marriages when he says: "Through the wrongs done by the violators of the family in creating the intermixing of classes, the eternal *dharmas* of caste and family are destroyed" (1.43). While it is unclear how much emphasis to put on this since these are Arjuna's (and not Krishna's) words, I think the system of class and caste plays a central role in the *Gita* since it provides at least one of the principal contexts for the development of one's *dharma* or moral, social, and familial duties.

Brahman

Brahman (sometimes understood as the all-encompassing omnipotent and omniscient God) is taken to be the pure eternal ageless principle that is foundational in explaining the nature and end of our universe. *Brahman* exists in each living being and is the only part that is eternal or true about us. The Sanskrit term "atman" (translated as the self) is used to refer to the presence of *Brahman* in each one of us. *Brahman* exists in each one of us, according to the Hindus, in the sense that a representation of this pure principle exists in us. The *Gita* refashions this concept of *Brahman* in a number of interesting ways. As it will be noted shortly, *Brahman* is personalized by being subsumed within the divine being of Krishna. In the words of Phillips, "the *Gita* has *Brahman*, the Absolute, as active, making *dharma*, patterns of right action, including social justice, out there in the world" (2009, 101). Moreover, unlike the Upanishads where *Brahman* is characterized in terms of its "pure-consciousness" and therefore its "self manifested" nature, the *Gita* describes *Brahman* most commonly as the "unthinkable," "unchangeable," and the "unmanifested" (Dasgupta 1975, 471). This is also how the Upanishadic absolute *Brahman* is used at times in the *Gita* to refer to Krishna's lower nature or Prakriti, the material and substratum of all change in the universe. Thus, following Edgerton (1972), we could argue that a certain "dethronement of the [pure principle of] Brahman" happens in the *Gita* through which it becomes humanized and contextualized.

The philosophy of the *Gita*

I have already mentioned that the unique strength of the *Gita* lies in its ability to synthesize and harmonize many of the disparate and divergent ideas and themes of its time. In the moral context of how one should live one's life, the *Gita* synthesizes elements of the orthodoxy of prescribed action with elements of heterodoxy that makes attaining liberation (*sannyasa* or renunciation) from the cycle of birth and rebirth the final goal of human life. In the context of the practice of the Hindu religion, the *Gita* synthesizes the "social polytheism" of Vedic orthodoxy with Upanishadic monism, thus resulting in a "personal monotheism" or a "non-dualistic theism." Finally, in developing its philosophy, the *Gita* focuses on the relationship between everyday reality and the ultimate reality and synthesizes the dualism of early Samkhya philosophy with a "personalized monism" resulting in a personal non-dualism (see also Phillips 2009, 101). In its philosophy the *Gita* also provides "means by which one can go beyond believing and conceiving" one's relation to and identity with the ultimate reality to "actually experiencing or realizing" that union (Patel 1991, 14). These means are laid out in the *yoga* of knowledge (jnana), the *yoga* of action (karma), and the *yoga* of devotion (bhakti).

The first chapter of the *Gita* opens with Arjuna, who, when faced with the prospect of fighting and possibly killing his extended family, becomes dejected and declares, "I will not fight." He summons Krishna, calling into question the need to fight to win kingdoms in order to share with family. If the price of such a victory is the blood of one's near and dear relatives, then what is the point of such a war? That is Arjuna's dilemma. The rest of the *Gita* is devoted to Krishna's response to Arjuna wherein Krishna explains the importance of the battle and convinces Arjuna to fight. The short answer to Arjuna's dilemma is that Arjuna must fight, not only because as a member of the Kshatriya class it is his dharma or duty, but also because irrespective of class or caste, one must disregard any expected or planned outcome when performing a duty. Further, Krishna also chides Arjuna because the very source of his dilemma is unfounded:

> You grieve for those who should not be grieved for and yet speak as do the wise. Wise men grieve neither for the dead nor for the living. There never was a time when I was not, nor you, nor even these rulers of men. Nor will there be a time in future when any of us will cease to be. Just as the dweller of this body passes through childhood, youth and old age, so does it pass into another body. This does not confuse the wise. (2.11–13)

Krishna's larger argument here revolves around the nature of the individual, the nature of the universe, and the resulting purpose of human life. Krishna argues that the most important aspect of every individual or embodied self is immortal because it is in reality a part of Krishna himself (15.7). In the course of his counsel, Krishna also reveals that he is the ultimate reality of the universe (thus incorporating the Upanishadic notion of *Brahman*). Also in the fashion of Upanishadic thinkers, the ultimate goal of human life is described as realizing one's identity with the ultimate truth, namely, Krishna. According to Krishna, this is what constitutes human salvation or liberation. Finally as a means for attaining this moksa or liberation, Krishna contends there are at least three different ways in which Krishna's multifaceted *yoga* can be described.

What grounds the ethics of the three *yoga*s is the metaphysics of the *Gita*, namely, what the *Gita* has to say about the nature and constitution of our world, including ourselves. In developing its metaphysics the *Gita* draws on the dualistic metaphysics of Samkhya[6] consisting of Prakriti (commonly translated as "nature" or "matter") and Purusha (commonly translated as "spirit," "soul," or "consciousness"). Samkhya presents a system of cosmic evolution where everything that comes into existence evolves through an interaction between these two principles. While the matter of everything, and therefore the substratum for action or change, is provided by Prakriti, an infinite number of Purushas, which are in reality eternally unchanging, provide the basis for numerous embodied selves. Embodied self comes into being when the Purusha is made to mistakenly identify itself with the psycho-physical body it finds itself in through the faculty of subjectification (*ahamkara*). As a result it fatefully and deterministically comes to consider itself as the agent. The Purusha thus gets trapped in the world of deaths and rebirths through karma or the residual power of one's actions. This is the source of bondage in this universe, and freedom consists of Purusha realizing its true nature as completely separate from Prakriti.

The *Gita* utilizes the basic Samkhya categories. However, unlike the Samkhya, the *Gita* replaces the dualism of Prakriti and Purusha where these two principles are considered entirely independent by subsuming them under Krishna as his two natures: Prakriti as his "lower" nature, and Purusha as his "higher nature" (7.5). Further, unlike the numerous Purushas of the Samkhya, the *Gita* acknowledges one ultimate Purusha (*Purushottama*), namely, Krishna (15.18).

The metaphysics of the Gita: *Three* gunas

According to the *Gita* what allows the Prakriti to give rise to the myriad diversity in the world is its three constituents or the three *gunas*. Once again drawing upon the philosophical themes of the Samkhya, the *Gita* takes the *gunas* as ingredients with different properties associated with them, with which everything in this world, including us humans, is constructed. *Gunas* are "insentient psycho-physical constituents" posited as theoretical entities. They not only account for the myriad diversity of our reality but also provide the underlying mechanism that holds the universe in place. As Krishna says, "there is no creature either on earth or again among the gods in heaven who is free from these three *gunas*, born of Prakriti" (18.40). The Samkhya also uses the analogy of "strands" in discussing the *gunas*, thereby referring to the three *gunas* as three strands constituting the rope of Prakriti that binds everything to their material bondage. In being the constituents, the *gunas* are taken in the *Gita*, "not only as fields or dimensions of physical Nature, but also as qualities of psychic being and moral consciousness," thereby determining every individual's psychological dispositions as well as moral attitudes (Deutsch 1968, 13). There are three such *gunas*, namely:

Sattva (goodness) which is responsible for properties like lightness, illumination, truth, and knowledge;

Rajas (passion) which is responsible for properties like activity, energy, passion, and movement; and

Tamas (dark inertia) which is responsible for properties like lethargy, laziness, stupidity, and inertia.

Although each of these three *gunas* is present in each of us, the ratio in which they are present varies from individual to individual. For the sake of illustration, let us arbitrarily postulate that each individual is composed of a total of ten counts. We may now imagine a person who has seven counts of goodness, two counts of passion, and only one count of dark inertia. Comparing this person with someone who has one count of goodness, two counts of passion, and seven counts of dark inertia—once again arbitrarily speaking—we might be able to reflect on how the behavior of these two individuals would differ. Since goodness is associated with light, illumination, and truth, if a person has prevalence of this *guna* over the other two *gunas* in one's constitution, then that person will definitely exhibit behavioral dispositions proper to that *guna*; they would, for example, quest for truth, have contemplative, moral attitudes, and an interest in knowing the Vedas.[7] On the other hand, since dark inertia is associated with lethargy, stupidity, and laziness, a person who has prevalence of this *guna* over the other two in his constitution would exhibit dark inertia-like behavioral traits and dispositions like laziness, inability to finish any complicated or sophisticated job, or even cultivation of base pleasures. Krishna uses this doctrine of *gunas* to provide a justification for all phenomenal variations and localized stabilities of time qualities that seem inherent in a substance over time.

It could be argued that at the time of one's death the ratio of good versus bad in one's associated karmic residue determines the constitution, i.e., the distribution of *gunas*, of the new being that is reborn. The *Gita* does not provide an exact mechanism through which the new distribution is determined. However, given that karmic residues are remnants of our actions, which in turn are shaped by our given dispositions, a certain determinism seems to follow. Deutsch describes the law of karma as maintaining "that every action (whether physical or mental) carries along with it determinants for future action" (1968, 182). In the *Gita* Krishna expresses a common belief of Hinduism that "the attitude of mind at the hour of death is particularly influential in determining man's state after death" (Edgerton 1972, 176); Krishna states, "whatever state of being a man remembers while leaving his body at the time of death, to that state alone he enters due to his ever persistence in it" (8.6). Admittedly part of the goal of Krishna's claim here is to highlight the prospect of a yogi (a practitioner of *yoga*) of devotion who by taking refuge in Krishna at the time of death ensures that he will be born in good circumstances (if he is reborn at all). However, it also seems to me that what is being suggested here is that, in terms of disposition, the tendencies and behavioral patterns one cultivates in a lifetime—drawing from one's constitution of *gunas*—most likely influence one's mental frame at the time of one's death, and so too determine one's next station. If one's mindset reflects a prevalence of goodness over passion and dark inertia, then one's natural disposition is to become a Brahmin by being reborn as a Brahmin, i.e., as a son of a Brahmin father. Thus in this society idealized by the *Mahabharata*, "one's identity is, as it were, a *fait accompli*, since the circumstances of one's birth dictate one's livelihood, and incidental individualities are put down to *karman* [karma] carried forward from past lives" (Brodbeck 2004, 94). What seems to be implied is that, if you find yourself as a Sudra, it is no one's fault but your own. The bad karma accumulated in your past lives created a bad constitution which can only be capable of performing Sudra duties.[8] Thus, "one is completely responsible for oneself. A man's present condition is the result of his past action over many lives, and his future condition will result from his past and present action" (Deutsch 1968, 13).[9] It is also this reasoning that could be taken to provide support for Krishna's persistent claim in the *Gita*: "One's own *dharma*, done imperfectly, is better than performing another's *dharma* well; better to die in one's own *dharma* for another's *dharma* is perilous" (3.35).

Let me also draw our attention briefly to the role of Krishna in the determinism of Prakriti. In spite of maintaining generally that "the arrangement of the world is due to the effect of *karma*," there are other passages (e.g., 14.19) in the *Gita* which "indicate that *karma* does not produce its effects by itself, but that God [Krishna] rewards or punishes good and bad deeds by arranging good and bad births associated with joys and sorrows" (Dasgupta 1975, 522). Therefore, while a determinism centered upon a theory of karma based on each embodied self's actions seems to dominate the *Gita*, it seems clear that the text does not reflect a completely consistent view on the working of the law of karma.

The **Gita** *and the periphery*

I noted earlier in the section "The *Gita* and the Evolution of Hinduism" the *Gita*'s prominent role in the remaking of Hinduism. What I now want to note is the historical context in which the *Gita* comes to play this role. As a number of interpreters have noted, until the late nineteenth century the *Gita* "was not really a popular scripture in India" and that "it was known mainly to the spiritual elite who treated it as another Upanishad" (Neufeldt in Minor 1986, 11). However this state of affairs seems to change quickly starting in early twentieth century when the *Gita* "came to occupy a position (which in the popular mind it has since that day never lost) as the undisputed statement of all that is most central and most important in the Hindu world of ideas" (Robinson 2006, 5 is quoting Sharpe). Robinson also mentions Arvind Sharma's comment in this regard that the *Gita* since became "the most significant text of modern Hinduism." While a complex set of factors contributed to this changed fortune of the *Gita*, for my purpose here I want to focus on how it allowed the recreation of India's golden past. This is most evident in the nationalist adoption of the *Gita* by the early twentieth-century Indian independence movement. Such a distinctly political and nationalist tone is present in Radhakrishnan's commentary where "the *Gita* becomes, ..., a document of Civil religion for the modern Indian nation-state, and it embodies the values of idealism and the spiritual life that India is able to provide to the 'technological' and 'materialist' West" (Larson 1981, 525). Given this ascendance of the *Gita* to becoming the "Bible" of Hinduism, it seems important to explore what the *Gita* has to say and is taken to say about various groups of people assigned to the periphery by the socio-political and cultural structures of Hinduism and India.

Here I want to focus on the *Gita*'s take on women and a response to the *Gita* from Ambedkar, the most prominent leader of the Dalit community of India.

Women and the *Gita*

There are only two verses in the *Gita* that mention women. In 1.41, Arjuna argues, "O Krishna, when *adharma* prevails, the women of the family are corrupted and from the corruption of women, O Varshneya, the intermixture of class arises." Here Arjuna could be taken to reflect a societal anxiety that seems to correlate purity (or corruption) of women to stability and order. In 9.32 Krishna comments that those who take refuge in him can reach the highest goal *even if* they are "born of sinful wombs," namely, "women, members of the vaisya caste (business caste) or even a member of the sudra caste (servant caste)." Given just these two mentions of women, the *Gita* could be taken to have rather little to say about women. However, the *Gita* plays a far more significant role in determining a response to the "women's question." When discussing women's experience in India in the nineteenth and twentieth centuries, what post-colonial theorists like Partha Chatterjee call the "women's question" can serve as a point of departure. This concept features prominently in the discourse around modernity within the colonial context of British India. What is typically referred to by the "women's question" is the phenomenon where women—their socio-economic conditions and plights—are viewed as location, indeed ground zero, for the modernist discourse. In British India, this location was conceived in terms of a debate between colonial orientalists and traditional nationalists. While the orientalist perspective argued for reforming and changing the conditions of Indian women, the nationalist rhetoric opposed such arguments by creating a glorification of India's past. More specifically, as Lata Mani notes, women became "emblematic of tradition and the reworking of tradition" was done through "debating their rights and status in society" (1989, 121). The *Gita* played a central role in this "reworking" as it came to be viewed as the "essence" of Hindu scriptures and its authority came to be "considered as most sacred by Hindus of all persuasions" (Robinson 2006, 5 quoting Raja Ram Mohan Roy). So even though the *Gita* directly doesn't say much on women, it plays an important role in creating a version of what it means to be a traditional Hindu woman.

Ambedkar and the *Gita*

Dr. B. R. Ambedkar, the Chairman of the Drafting Committee of the Indian Constitution, grew up as a member of Mahar, one of the numerous communities considered untouchable by caste Hindus. In his "Krishna and his Gita" (2002) Ambedkar offers a spirited criticism of the *Gita*. According to him, "What the *Bhagvad Gita* does is to defend certain dogmas of religion on philosophic grounds" (2002, 193). Ambedkar takes the *Gita* to be a post-Buddhist text conceived by the upper caste Hindu men in response to Buddha's critique of the Brahmanical Hinduism. His main critique consists of two arguments: first that the *Gita*'s defense of the *yoga* of action is truly a defense of the Vedic ritualism. As he writes, "By Karma marga the *Bhagvad Gita* means the performance of the observances, such as *Yojnas* as a way to salvation" (Ambedkar 2002, 194). The other dogmas that Ambedkar critiques is what he takes to be the *Gita*'s defense of the caste system (2002, 195). He thus takes the *Gita* to be a text that is fundamentally against the lower castes and especially the untouchables. While some others have also maintained this line against the *Gita*, I think Ambedkar is the strongest defender of this line of criticism. The main argument presented in response to Ambedkar's attack notes that the *Gita* ultimately shows us why the caste differences are not important. As Dnyaneshwar, the founder of the Bhakti sect in the Marathi speaking areas, takes Krishna to be saying in his "commentary on the *Bhagavad Gita*, the *Dnyaneshwari*":

> There is a distinction between the Khaira and the Chandana trees only so long as they are not put into fire; but as soon as they are put inside it, they become one with it, and the distinction between them vanishes. Similarly, the Kshatriya, the Vaisyas, the Sudras and Women are so called only as long as they have not reached Me. But having reached Me, they cease to be distinguished; as salt becomes one with the ocean, even so they become one with Me. (Zelliot 2001, 22 quoting Dnyaneshwar; see also Nadkarni 2017, 233)

The ethics of the yogas

A Sudra or an outcaste might now ask, "is there any hope for me?" Krishna would respond, "yes, of course since liberation or moksa is not confined to any particular class or caste." Anybody who practices an appropriate *yoga* properly would come close to attaining liberation. The Sanskrit term *yoga*, being derived from the root "yuj," which commonly means "to yoke," or "to unite or join oneself with," means union or even balance. In the *Gita, yoga* is sometimes used "to mean the controlling of one's lower sensuous nature and the realization of one's higher spiritual nature" (Deutsch 1968, 6). *Yoga* in the *Gita* thus stands not only for the ultimate union between individual embodied self and Krishna but also for the process of controlling the mind and the senses which prepares one for the ultimate union. A practitioner of *yoga* is prescribed the golden middle course of moderate food, drink, sleep, and movement in the *Gita*. The object of such a practitioner "is not the absolute destruction of the mind, but to bring the mind or the ordinary self into communion with the higher self" or Krishna (Dasgupta 1975, 448).

Krishna talks about three *yoga*s—of Jnana or knowledge, Karma or action and Bhakti or devotion[10]—in the *Gita* and purports to describe them as three different routes to the same summit, namely, becoming one with Krishna. While discussing the "ethics" of the *yoga*, I need to acknowledge that in the existing literature of comparative philosophy an almost exclusive focus has been aimed at the *yoga* of karma or action. One might be able to articulate several reasons for this emphasis: given the dominant trend in Western ethical discussions to focus on human action, the *yoga* that focuses on action would naturally be of interest. But even more importantly, the *Gita*'s karma *yoga* of non-attached action also makes it an obvious candidate for comparison with Kantian deontological ethics.[11] However, this narrow focus on the *yoga* of action in discussing the ethics of the *Gita* distracts us from appreciating the relevance of other two *yoga*s that the *Gita* proposes. This also ignores the organic context of the *Gita*'s ethics and reflects selective interest in the *Gita*'s philosophy motivated from a Eurocentric attitude. Furthermore, it keeps us from articulating some problematic implications of the *yoga* of action and the *Gita*'s unique contribution to the philosophy of action. If we consider all three *yoga*s as relevant from the perspective of ethics, we also come to realize the centrality of the notion of *samatva* or sameness and equanimity for the *Gita*. Since this equanimity is articulated as the foundational virtue that needs to be cultivated for a successful practice of each of the three *yoga*s, this focus allows us to detect strong elements of virtue ethics in the *Gita*. In fact, the *Gita*'s unique contribution in this regard is found in the fact that duty and virtue are viewed as complementary, rather than incompatible, in the *Gita* (Gupta 2006, 395). Equanimity as a central aspect of this ethics of *yoga* also draws our attention to an emergent characteristic of this ethical theory: if we understand equanimity as going beyond the pairs of opposites inherent to physical, psychological, and moral dualities, then the goal of the *Gita* seems to be to realize a kind of trans-morality where agency ultimately fades away. If agency presupposes the separation between the doer and the doing, and if morality is inextricably tied to agency then a loss of agency would also mean a transcendence of morality at least in this most common sense.

The yoga of knowledge

One might ask, what kind of knowledge would help me attain liberation? Would this be factual knowledge like *the cup on my desk is blue*, or conceptual knowledge like *all bachelors are indeed unmarried men*? Krishna replies that it is neither, since what one needs to know is not something external but rather one's own inner life and internal theater of being, one's own self. Krishna says,

> But for whom that ignorance is destroyed by the knowledge of the self, their knowledge illumines that supreme (reality) like the sun. Comprehending that, their self focused on that, being supremely devoted to that, with that being their final goal, they go to a state beyond return, having their sins destroyed by knowledge. (5.16–17)

How does the yogi of knowledge arrive at this state that is "beyond return"? Krishna argues that this *yoga* "demands a rigorous intellectual discrimination between the phenomenal world and the real world of Brahman, and culminates in an intuitive identification which shatters the independent existence of everything but the non-dual one" (Deutsch 1968, 15). This is how renunciation or *sannyasa* happens. According to Krishna, sin happens only when we act from our desires, anger, passion, and attachments. This is the same as acting without knowledge because if we knew our real nature or the true nature of our self, we would not act in such a fashion. So true knowledge takes us beyond sin, but what happens when we arrive at this state of knowing? Here the power of perfect knowledge results in a withdrawal from the world, either in the sense of renunciation of prescribed ritualistic actions or in the sense of renunciation of the fruits of actions. The *yoga* of knowledge thus reflects the *Gita's* adoption of the Upanishadic focus on "intuitional perception" as a way of attaining release.

The yoga of action

The *yoga* of action requires one to perform an action for the pure reason that it is one's duty and without thinking of the outcome of that action. It is like helping an elderly person because it is one's duty and not because the elderly person might help you get elected to the city council. Again, in the words of the *Gita*:

> You have claim over your actions alone and never over the fruits of action. Never live for the fruits of action nor attach yourself to inaction. O Dhananjaya (Arjuna)! Perform actions being firm in *yoga*, having abandoned attachments; be impartial to success and failure, for this equanimity is called *yoga*. (2.47–48)

What is wrong with attachment? Attachment to things and people forces us to act out of desire and selfishness, which continues our bondage. Impartiality or indifference here does not mean apathy or lack of concern, but rather that when one knows the true nature of reality, one follows with unbiased and disinterested reason into action. Why avoid inaction too? Simply because we cannot deny action. It is our body's nature. Even when we think we are in deep sleep, and therefore inactive, our heart and kidneys are still functioning. When Arjuna asks Krishna which one is better, the *yoga* of knowledge, i.e., renunciation of action, or the *yoga* of action, Krishna clarifies that while both deliver the same outcome, his preference is for the *yoga* of action because renunciation is hard to attain without the *yoga* of action (5.6). In fact, on numerous occasions in the *Gita* the *yoga* of action is repeatedly praised and favored. The *Gita's* emphasis on the *yoga* of action underscores its author's proposed synthesis between orthodox ritualism and an Upanishadic focus on complete renunciation of all action. What allows this synthesis is a unique extension to the law of karma that transforms it into the *yoga* of action. Thus Krishna offers a "two-pronged" argument for the *yoga* of action:

> [H]e defends the right kind of action against, on the one hand, the overzealous advocates of Vedic ritualism and, on the other, the propounders of the doctrine that all acts should be given up. His argument is at once simple and complex: simple, because he finds cause to propose that action is both necessary and unproductive of rebirth; complex, because he attempts to hold on to the orthodoxy of social action while revolutionizing it from within, and at the same time to demolish the heterodoxy of renunciation-at-any-price without discarding the value of renunciation per se. (van Buitenen 1981, 16–17)

In spite of its seeming simplicity the goal of non-attached action presents a paradox to philosophers. The *Gita* appears inconsistent since on the one hand it recommends non-attached actions because they ultimately deliver us from bondage, but it also wants us to perform our action without any desire for a goal or outcome. Arindam Chakrabarti (1988) clarifies that the *Gita* and Kant can both be taken to ask us not to act for the sake of happiness or ultimate deliverance, but to act from duty "for *being worthy* of happiness [or of deliverance]," i.e., "with the *hope* but not *desire* for it" (Chakrabarti 1988, 333). Still, if the *Gita* is asking us to perform actions without desires then what is the psychology of such actions? Especially given our ordinary understanding of voluntary actions as originating in desires or intentions, is the *Gita* asking us to renounce and therefore refrain from actions altogether? As noted previously, the *Gita* clearly rejects this reading not only because complete renunciation of action is impossible given the nature of the physical universe that includes the psycho-physical complex of the human body, but also because the *Gita* seems to argue that prescribed actions should be performed for the maintenance of social order and stability. Thus the *Gita* does not ask us to renounce actions, but only our attachment to the fruits of such actions. What allows the *Gita* to maintain this position is a theorization of agency using its metaphysics of the *gunas*. In this "behavioral analysis of action," agency itself is theorized away. Thus the *Gita* argues, "the cause of action is never an independent human being, but is always *prakriti*, the material world as a whole, of which any individual person is an arbitrary subsection. The teleological view of actions as initiated and owned by individuals is, ..., a mistake" (Brodbeck 2004, 89).[12]

Another dimension of this metaphysics is realizing the determinism that follows from Prakriti because "[n]o one, indeed, can exist even for a moment without performing action; for everyone is helplessly made to act by the *gunas* born of Prakriti" (3.5). "Action is inevitable because it is material nature [Prakriti] that acts, thru the power of past actions which compel future actions as their result" (Edgerton 1972, 160–161). But in this metaphysics, one might argue, lies the problem of psychology. The fact that Purusha or atman is argued to be unchanging and unchangeable makes it impossible for it to participate in the machinery of action. In laying out the steps to practicing the *yoga* of action the *Gita* requires us to make the intellect or buddhi "unitary, concentrated and resolute." But since the entire mental complex, including the intellect, operates within the domain of Prakriti for the *Gita*, "if *prakriti* governs the actions that Arjuna will do, then it must also govern whether or not he will do those actions without attachment" (Brodbeck 2004, 98). Arjuna has as little control over attachment to actions as actions themselves. Thus in spite of the emphasis the *Gita* places on the *yoga* of non-attached action, Brodbeck concludes, "the only way out is to realize that our mental state, the internal tone of our experience, is, like our actions, absolutely, none of our business" (2004, 101). However, this deterministic gloss is by no means the only or the most preferred reading among the commentators and scholars of the *Gita*. Abhinavagupta, a tenth-century commentator from the Kashmiri Shaiva tradition, emphasized that instead of adopting the sharp dualism between Prakriti and Purusha and the determinism that follows, there is a way to resolve the impasse between the "prakritic determinism" and voluntary action. By choosing to offer one's action to something other than oneself—to *Brahman* or Krishna—one is able to attain the dual consciousness of Krishna as timeless *Brahman* as well as the actor in the world creating dharma. Furthermore, Abhinavagupta continues that we, as parts of Shiva (who he equates with Krishna), share in Shiva's freedom and power of self-determination.[13] The plausibility of this reading also follows from the fact that Krishna contends that Prakriti and Purusha are two aspects of his nature and not two irreducible categories.

The yoga of devotion

A few moments' reflection allows us to realize that both the *yoga*s of action and knowledge are very difficult, if not impossible. How many of us can devote ourselves to the life of pure introspective contemplation or of pure disinterested actions? Moreover, the apparent unavailability of the technique of non-attachment might suggest an internal inconsistency within the *Gita*'s formulation of the *yoga* of action. However, Krishna would ask us not to worry since there is this third way, the *yoga* of devotion, which the *Gita* not only acknowledges for the first time as an additional path alongside the *yoga*s of knowledge and action, but also offers as the most relevant *yoga*. What does the *yoga* of devotion require? It does not require anything else except complete surrender and loyalty to the object of one's devotion, in this case Krishna. Thus Krishna says to Arjuna, "Focus your mind on me, be my devotee, sacrifice to me, bow to me; having thus disciplined yourself, taking me as the highest goal, you will come only to me" (9.34). It is also important to consider Krishna's comments that even an extremely wicked person becomes a saint when he devotes himself to Krishna (9.30–32), or, that he rescues his devotees, i.e., those who follow the *yoga* of devotion "from the ocean of recurring deaths" (12.7). Do these statements suggest that practice of the *yoga* of devotion neutralizes or cancels a devotee's karmic residues, hastening his or her union with *Brahman*? Edgerton seems to think so when he writes, "God [Krishna], as it were, cancels the laws of nature for the benefit of his devoted worshipers, and brings them to salvation by divine grace" (1972, 174). Apart from hinting at the role of grace in one's freedom, these comments also work together to elevate the importance of the *yoga* of devotion within the overall message of the *Gita*.

The introduction of the *yoga* of devotion also allows the *Gita* to celebrate a personal God as the center of the practiced faith of Hinduism. Indeed, this is what allows the *Gita* to harmonize the polytheism consisting of many gods and goddesses of early Vedic Hinduism and the monism of one ultimate unchanging principle of Upanishadic Hinduism and fashion its own distinctive brand of monotheism of a God whose name was Krishna. As van Buitenen remarks,

> *Bhakti* [devotion], then, appears as a form of religiosity specifically Hindu in that it allows a religious man to create out of a social polytheism a personal monotheism. While he becomes ever more firmly a monotheist, the surrounding polytheism will continue to provide the believer, by the old process of henotheism,[14] with metaphors for the supremacy of his god. Other gods become God's servants, or components imaginable in God's manifestations, or forms God assumed in his periodic incarnations. Whole pantheons now exist for God's glorification, so that the believer may stride through his world and discern that those who worship other gods are in fact engaged in the worship of an embodiment of *his* God, and therefore need not be disturbed in their simple faith. (1981, 25)

As mentioned earlier, in the *Gita* the different *yoga*s are sometimes seen as merely different ways of attaining the same result. Given that they all aspire for the same goal and share the basic assumption about human predicament, they are all interwoven into each other. However, does the *Gita* promote them all equally? It does not seem so, since it could be argued, as van Buitenen and Deutsch, among others, have argued, that the *yoga* of knowledge is underemphasized in relation to the *yoga* of action and the *yoga* of devotion. In fact, at times the *Gita* seems to argue that there is identity between the *yoga*s of knowledge or renunciation and action. As Krishna says, "One, who performs actions that are required (by the scriptures) without depending on the fruit of action, is a renouncer and a yogi; not one who maintains no ritual fires and performs no rites" (6.1). Once again Krishna is offering a synthesis here between action and renunciation by suggesting that it is not acting itself that imprisons one; rather, it is acting without true knowledge, i.e., with a sense of ego, wherein one considers oneself as the agent, that imprisons one. It is also in tune with the *Gita*'s general attitude of world-affirmation where maintaining the social (and moral) order is one of the most pressing needs. However, in the final analysis, the *yoga* of devotion comes to capture the *Gita*'s unique ethos. Through devotion, Krishna "supplants the stoicism [of knowledge] with the enthusiasm of the believer acting in God's name and for his glorification, and replaces the salvation-seeking knowledge with that knowledge of God that only *bhakti* [devotion] can bring" (van Buitenen 1981, 29). *Bhakti* (devotion) thus comes to complete and complement the *karma yoga* teaching of the *Gita*. I agree with Edgerton when he writes, "all these various ways are more or less vaguely blended and felt as in the last analysis essentially one; but the *devotional coloring is perhaps the most constant characteristic of the blend*" (1972, 175, emphasis added).

In conclusion, I would like to suggest that the unparalleled popularity of the *Gita* among Hindus even today and students of yoga is because of the diversity that the *Gita* acknowledges in paths to the final goal of *Brahman*. The *Gita* accepts that each of us is uniquely positioned in our own spiritual journeys and that the same means will not work for all. What is unique about the *Gita* among most of the religious texts of the world is that it accepts our diversity and offers various solutions that appeal to different intelligences. Most importantly, in its celebration of the *yoga* of devotion, the *Gita* resonates with the masses as it tries "to meet the 'man-in-the-street' half-way" (Edgerton 1972, 167). Thus, "the object of sense-control in the *Gita* is not the attainment of a state of emancipated oneness or the absolute cessation of all mental processes, but the more intelligible and common-sense ideal of the attainment of steadiness of mind, contentment and the power of entering into touch with God [Krishna]" (Dasgupta 1975, 492). The simplicity and clarity of the *Gita*'s message is embodied in the *caramasloka* ("last" verse) when Krishna says: "Relinquishing all *dharma*s, take refuge in me alone; do not grieve (for) I will free you from all evils" (18.66).

Notes

1 I thank Simon Brodbeck for pointing this out to me.

2 It is common to consider Krishna as a personification of the Hindu God Vishnu mainly because Arjuna addresses Krishna as "Vishnu" twice (11.24, 11.30) in the *Gita*. Deshpande also points out that in a number of places in the *Mahabharata* Krishna is identified with Vishnu (MB 5.47.82). However, other scholars including van Buitenen and Patel have argued that in the course of the *Gita* Krishna not only identifies himself with a number of other gods like Yama, Agni, Vayu, Prajapati, and Brahma (11.39), but also seems to present himself as the ultimate God par excellence (as *Purushottama* in 15.18; see also 11.18, 11.38). In this way the *Gita*'s Krishna is "suprasectarian" (van Buitenen 1981, 28).

3 While quoting verses from the *Gita* I have first given the chapter number followed by the verse number(s). Thus "4.7" refers to verse 7 from chapter 4.

4 This is also the ultimate goal of a Buddhist and Jain life.

5 In his essay titled "*Swabhava and Swadharma*," Aurobindo (1997) develops another way of interpreting the notions one's own nature and one's own duties (*svadharma*) that would counter my argument here. In this interpretation *svadharma* refers to one's own unique path to and relationship with the Divine and not the externally determined caste duties. However, since I can find very little textual support in the *Gita* for Aurobindo's proposed interpretation, I find his argument ultimately unconvincing. I thank Stephen Phillips for drawing my attention to this essay by Aurobindo.

6 The ancient teachings of Samkhya later received its definitive form in the *Samkhya-Karika* of Isvarakrishna in fourth century CE and are thereby considered the first formulation of the classical Samkhya school of philosophy.

7 In chapter 17 of the *Gita* while outlining the three-fold faiths, Krishna aligns them closely to the three *gunas* in terms of dispositions. For example, certain "savory, smooth [and] firm" foods that promote longevity, energy, and health, among other things, are preferred, Krishna argues, by "men of goodness" (17.8). This discussion gives a strong indication that *gunas* are taken here as manifesting themselves as dispositions or even preferences.

8 For this reason Dasgupta argues that the possibility of a Sudra performing sacrifices or *tapas* (austerity) or the study of the Vedas would be "opposed by the *Gita* as it would be against the prescribed caste-duties" (1975, 514).

9   Brodbeck (2004) raises some interesting questions about
        the scope of this freedom especially within the "prakritic"
        determinism of the *Gita* and the possibility of non-attached action
        within this scope. See the discussion on the *yoga* of action below.

10   Though these are the most prominent *yoga*s that Krishna
        discusses in the *Gita*, he also mentions *buddhi yoga* (for example
        in 2.49 and 10.10) which can be understood as the "yoga for the
        higher rationality" (Phillips 2009, 179). The goal of this *yoga* is the
        same as the other three, namely, an ultimate union with Krishna.

11   However, I have argued elsewhere (Maitra 2006) that while such
        a comparison is useful in drawing out many of the philosophical
        contexts and presuppositions of these two moral theories, any
        attempted one-to-one correspondence between the two would be
        hard to find. While Kant's theory is situated in the enlightenment
        egalitarianism, in the *Gita* the most important *dharmas* (moral
        duties) are given in the social and familial contexts. Further, while
        the *Gita* strives to transcend the very sense of agency, no such
        urgency troubles Kant. On the contrary, cultivation of agency is at
        the heart of moral engagement for Kant.

12   Using a similar kind of analysis of the *Gita*'s *yoga* of action,
        Teschner (1992) has argued that it is the "phenomenology of
        action" that is of primary importance in the *Gita*.

13   I thank Stephen Phillips for helping me appreciate this point.

14   "Henotheism" is a term popularized by Max Muller which means
        worshipping a single God while accepting the existence or
        possible existence of other deities.

1

Arjuna's Sorrow[1]

Summary

The chapter opens with a request from the blind king Dhritarashtra to Sanjaya to provide an eyewitness account of everything that takes place in the battlefield of Kurukshetra. Sanjaya's account begins by identifying the main fighters on both sides and also by capturing the charged atmosphere of the impending war. The long list of names of heroes with their war exploits that Sanjaya recounts seems to indicate the enormity of Arjuna's undertaking and fierceness of the imminent battle. Against this intense backdrop Arjuna's mental turmoil arises. Given that the war would require him to kill his own kinsmen, Arjuna wonders how his participation might be justified. In a consequentialist fashion he enumerates all the terrible outcomes of such a war. The chapter concludes with Arjuna's declaration that he will not fight.

Dhritarashtra said:

O Sanjaya, what did my men and the sons of Pandu do when they assembled, eager for battle, on the field of *dharma*—on the field of Kuru? (1)

Sanjaya said:

Seeing the army of the sons of Pandu arrayed, Duryodhana, the king, then approached his teacher (Drona) and said these words: (2)

"O teacher, behold this great army of the sons of Pandu, arranged in battle formation by the son of Drupada, your own skillful pupil. (3)

Here are heroes, mighty archers equal to Bhima and Arjuna in warfare—Yuyudhana, Virata and the great chariot-warrior Drupada. (4)

Also here are Dhristaketu, Chekitana and the powerful king of Kashi; Purujit, Kuntibhoja and Shaibya—bull among men. (5)

The valorous Yudhamanyu and the brave Uttamaujas; also the son of Subhadra and the sons of Draupadi—all indeed great chariot-warriors. (6)

Now, O best among the twice-born (Brahmin: member of the priest caste), know those that are outstanding on our side, the leaders of my army. In order to name them, I will declare them to you. (7)

They are your venerable self, and Bhishma and Karna, and Kripa—the victorious in battle; also are Ashvatthama (son of Drona) and Vikarna and the son of Somadatta. (8)

And there are many other heroes who have risked their lives for my sake; armed with various weapons, they are all skilled in warfare. (9)

Guarded by Bhishma, the strength of our army is unlimited, whereas protected by Bhima, the strength of their (Pandava) army is limited.[2] (10)

Therefore, in all the movements of the battle, all of you, stationed in your respective positions, must protect Bhishma alone, by any means." (11)

The valiant elder of the Kurus, the glorious grandsire (Bhishma) roared his lion's roar loudly and blew his conch horn to cause Duryodhana's delight. (12)

Then quite suddenly conches, kettledrums, cymbals, tabors and trumpets were sounded at once and the sound was tremendous. (13)

Then, standing on their magnificent chariot yoked with white stallions, Madhava (Krishna) and the son of Pandu (Arjuna) also sounded their divine conches. (14)

Hrishikesha (Krishna) blew Panchajanya (won from a demon), Dhananjaya (Arjuna) blew Devadatta (a gift of the gods), and the wolf-bellied, doer of terrible deeds (Bhima) blew his great conch Paundra. (15)

King Yudhisthira, the son of Kunti, blew his conch Anantavijaya (conch of boundless victory); Nakula and Sahadeva (his twin brothers) blew Sughosha (resonant conch) and Manipushpaka (jewel toned conch). (16)

The King of Kashi, a great archer, and Shikhandi, the great chariot-warrior; Dhrishtadyumna and Virata, and Satyaki—the undefeated, all blew their conches. (17)

O lord of the earth (Dhritarashtra), Drupada along with all the sons of Draupadi, and the mighty-armed son of Subhadra, all blew their respective conches. (18)

The tumultuous uproar, resounding through earth and sky, tore at the hearts of Dhritarashtra's men. (19)

Then seeing Dhritarashtra's men assembled, as weapons were about to be clashed, the son of Pandu, whose war flag bore the image of a monkey, lifted his bow. (20)

Then, O lord of the earth, he spoke these words to Hrishikesha: "O Achyuta, draw up my chariot between the two armies. (21)

So that I may see these men standing here eager for battle and know with whom I must fight in this enterprise of war. (22)

So that I may see those who are assembled here eager to fight, eager to accomplish in battle what is dear to the evil-minded son of Dhritarashtra." (23)

Sanjaya said:

O Bharata, thus asked by Gudakesha (Arjuna), Hrishikesha drew their magnificent chariot between the two armies. (24)

Facing Bhishma and Drona and all the rulers of the earth, he said: "O son of Pritha (Arjuna)! Behold the Kurus gathered here!" (25)

The son of Pritha saw there standing before him fathers, grandfathers, teachers and uncles, brothers, sons and grandsons and many friends, too. (26)

He also saw fathers-in-law and well-wishers in both armies. The son of Kunti (Arjuna), saw all his kinsmen thus present. (27)

Filled with deep pity, he said this in grief: "O Krishna, seeing my kinsmen gathered here eager to fight; (28)

My limbs sink and my mouth dries up, my body shivers and the hair stands on my flesh. (29)

Gandiva (the great bow) slips from my hand and even my skin burns all over; I am unable to stand still and my mind seems to reel. (30)

O handsome-haired one, I see adverse omens; and I don't see any good from killing my kinsmen in battle. (31)

O Krishna, I desire no victory, or a kingdom, or even pleasures; Of what use to us are kingdoms, or enjoyment or even life, O Govinda? (32)

For whose sake we desire kingdom, enjoyments and comforts, they stand here in battle, having surrendered their lives and fortunes. (33)

Teachers, fathers, sons and grandfathers as well; maternal uncles, fathers-in-law, grandsons, brothers-in-law and other relatives. (34)

O slayer of demon Madhu, I do not wish to slay them even if they slay me, not even for the kingship of three worlds, much less for this earth! (35)

O Janardana, what joy will come to us from killing the men of Dhritarashtra? Only sin would accrue to us if we kill these aggressors. (36)

O Madhava, therefore, it would not be right for us to kill the men of Dhritarashtra, our own kinsmen. How could we be happy after we kill our own people? (37)

This is so even though they see no wrong in destroying their family and no sin in injuring a friend because their reason is distorted by greed. (38)

How can we not be wise to turn away from this sin when we see clearly the sin of family destruction, O Janardana? (39)

The timeless family *dharma*s are lost in the destruction of family. When *dharma* is lost, *adharma* overwhelms the entire family. (40)

O Krishna, when *adharma* prevails, the women of the family are corrupted, and from the corruption of women, O Varshneya, the intermixture of class arises. (41)

This intermixture leads only to hell both for the family and the destroyers of family, for the ancestors fall to hell when the rites of Pindodaka (offering of rice and water) lapse. (42)

Through the wrongs done by the violators of the family in creating the intermixing of classes, the eternal *dharma*s of caste and family are destroyed. (43)

O Janardana, we have heard that those who destroy the family *dharmas* necessarily live in hell. (44)

Alas! We seem to be resolved to commit great sin in being ready to kill our kinsmen out of greed for the pleasure of a kingdom. (45)

It would indeed be better for me if the sons of Dhritarashtra with weapons in their hands kill me in battle when I am unarmed and unresisting." (46)

Sanjaya said:

Having spoken thus at the time of war, Arjuna sat down on the seat of the chariot; letting his bow and arrows fall, his mind overwhelmed with grief. (47)

Philosopher's corner: Chapter analysis and questions for consideration

The opening chapter of the *Gita* has often been regarded as unrewarding for philosophers because not much of philosophical relevance seems to take place. There is some truth to this estimation since much of this chapter is taken up with capturing the reality of Arjuna's dilemma in its dramatic force. However, this chapter provides at least two occasions for philosophical reflection—in terms of both comparative philosophy and Indian philosophy.

First, an opportunity arises to compare the thought conveyed with the contemporary ethical perspective of care ethics. Developed as a response to rule-based ethics, care ethics focuses on incorporating our relationships into ethical deliberations. When Arjuna asks, "How could we be happy after we kill our own people?" (1.37) he could be taken to be deliberating from a care perspective. Viewed in this light of care ethics, Arjuna's dilemma no longer remains a mere excuse for Krishna's discourse, but becomes a very relatable moral dilemma. Even after acknowledging the moral dimension of Arjuna's dilemma, a few interesting questions linger especially given the fact that his relationships seem to have varying moral relevance. For example, while from a care perspective any relationship can have moral relevance, the relationships that seem most troubling to Arjuna are given in a familial context—"fathers, grandfathers, teachers and uncles, brothers, sons and grandsons and many friends, too" (1.26)—as enumerated by Arjuna. Exploring the prioritization of relationships within the contemporary context of care ethics might be an interesting discussion topic for a student of the *Gita* to explore. The second occasion of potential philosophical engagement is Arjuna's claim that "when *adharma* prevails, the women of the family are corrupted, and from the corruption of women intermixture of class arises" (1.41). Of course Arjuna has just identified this *adharma* as "destruction of family" (1.40) by which he means killing one's own kinsmen. However, the exact causal mechanism through which destruction of family results in "women's corruption" remains a fertile topic for philosophical exploration. The last part of the verse, which takes intermixture of class to result from women's corruption, could also lead to an interesting discussion of the nature and extent of women's agency in the Hindu society and under what circumstances such agency could be put to action.

Some commentators take chapter 1 of the *Gita* to say a great deal about the morality of war and to outline two contrasting points of view on war, namely, that the *Gita* condones war for members of the Kshatriya caste especially if it is for a just cause; or, the alternative view famously ascribed to Gandhi where the *Gita* is taken to advocate for an inner war within each one of us between forces of good and evil instead of an external physical undertaking (see, for example, Diana Morrison's Introduction to chapter 1 in Easwaran 2007, 75–76). The proponents of the latter view also point to the opening verse where the battleground—the field of Kuru—is characterized as the field of *dharma*. Since each one of us faces the requirements of our own *dharma*, and the inner tensions that follow from such a demand, it seems natural that the *Gita* recommends a war for everyone. However, while this chapter surely sets the stage for such a debate, it does not explicitly engage with it. Finally, some interpreters of the *Gita* take this chapter to provide evidence for the claim that the *Gita* was a later addition to the core story of the *Mahabharata*. Since the focus and tone of all the chapters following this opening chapter are reflective, abstract, and speculative, the active and practical tone of this chapter is taken to substantiate the claim that this chapter serves as a bridge to insert the philosophical *Gita* into the war story of the *Mahabharata*. The narrative dynamics of this chapter in which Arjuna is in control could also be taken to provide further support for this. Arjuna is in control in asking his charioteer Krishna to position the chariot in the middle of the two armies (1.21) just as any warrior might ask of his charioteer. Arjuna is also in control in articulating the array of arguments that ultimately brings him to his paralyzing conclusion. This dynamics, as we will see shortly, is about to shift strikingly at the start of Chapter 2.

Notes

1 While the verses of the *Gita* are organized as chapters 23 through 40 of the sixth book of *Mahābhārata* (Bhandarkar Oriental Research Institute 1999), the chapters do not bear distinct titles. It is only in the editing of the *Gita* as a separate text that the chapter titles appear where each of the eighteen chapters is designated as a "type of yoga" (Chidbhavananda 1997, 32). Indeed, the present chapter is thus titled "*Arjuna-Vishada Yoga*" or the Yoga of Arjuna's Sorrow. However, since no specific *yoga* is discussed in this chapter, I have followed many other translators in leaving out the term "Yoga" from the title. In general, however, these titles work well in signaling the main theme of a chapter.

2 An alternative translation of this verse follows depending on how one translates the terms *aparyaptam* and *paryaptam*. Compare, for example, how Ramanuja, an eleventh-century eminent Vedanta philosopher and interpreter of the *Gita*, translates this verse: "Inadequate is the force of ours, which is guarded by Bhisma, while adequate is that force of theirs, which is guarded by Bhima" (Adidevananda 2009, 46; see also Edgerton 1972, 4).

2

The Yoga of Knowledge (and Philosophy)

Summary

The chapter opens with a restatement of Arjuna's worry. Arjuna argues even if he wins the battle his enjoyment of it would be smeared with the blood of his relatives and elders for whom he cares deeply. How can that be preferable? Krishna's main argument is developed in discernible stages. Responding to Arjuna's consequentialist worry Krishna offers a consequentialist response: given Arjuna's caste *dharma* as a Kshatriya, he must fight. Further, since abandoning the fight would harm his reputation as a great warrior, he should fight. Finally, if he gets killed in the war then he will gain heaven. If he wins then he stands to enjoy Earth. However, the force of Krishna's argument really lies in his trying to dispel the core reason for Arjuna's moral confusion, namely, a certain kind of attachment to outcomes. In this regard, Krishna's main argument consists of two claims. First, drawing upon the ontological distinction between the unreal and the real, Krishna argues that neither death nor birth should be agonized over. This claim assumes the further claim that the eternal aspect of every human being is indestructible. If one knows the eternal, everlasting nature of self and how our experience of pleasure and pain are generated, then those fleeting states of pleasure and pain will stop being the reason behind our actions. Ultimately, Krishna focuses on the role of desired outcomes in our action and counsels Arjuna "never [to] live for the fruits of action." Krishna also clarifies that merely knowing this truth is not sufficient. One needs to prepare one's mind and intellect by cultivating virtues like even-mindedness, equanimity, and steadfastness. This requires bringing the senses under control. An intellect thus trained is unshaken and is marked by its even-mindedness in success or failure. To cultivate such equanimity, or even-mindedness, and to thereby become a yogi, is the heart of Krishna's counsel.

Sanjaya said:

To him thus filled with pity, despondent, his eyes blurred with tears, the slayer of demon Madhu (Krishna) spoke these words. (1)

The blessed one (Krishna) said:

O Arjuna! Whence has this faintheartedness—unknown to honorable men, shameful and opposed to heaven—come upon you at this perilous moment? (2)

O son of Pritha (Arjuna)! Don't yield to powerlessness. It is unworthy of you. O scorcher of enemies (Arjuna), rejecting this petty weakness of heart, arise! (3)

Arjuna said:

O slayer of demon Madhu, how can I fight Bhishma and Drona with arrows on the battlefield, as, O slayer of the foes, they are worthy of my worship? (4)

It is better even to live on begged scraps of food in this world than to kill these noble-minded elders; because even though they are desirous of gain, having killed them I will have to enjoy pleasures smeared with their blood. (5)

Further, we don't know which is better for us: our conquering them or their conquering us. We should not want to live if we kill these men of Dhritarashtra arrayed before us. (6)

My very nature is overwhelmed by the fault of pity, my mind is confused about conflicting *dharma*; I ask you to tell me decisively which is better. I am your disciple; teach me as I have taken refuge in you. (7)

Indeed I don't see what could drive away the grief that withers my senses, even if I obtained unrivaled and prosperous kingdoms on earth and even sovereignty over gods. (8)

Sanjaya said:

Having spoken thus to Hrishikesha (Krishna), the conqueror of sleep, scorcher of enemies (Arjuna) said to Govinda (Krishna): "I will not fight" and he fell silent. (9)

O Bharata (Dhritarashtra), to him as he sat dejected in the midst of the two armies, Hrishikesha, as if mocking him gently, spoke these words: (10)

The blessed one (Krishna) said:

You grieve for those who should not be grieved for and yet speak as do the wise. Wise men grieve neither for the dead nor for the living. (11)

There never was a time when I was not, nor you, nor even these rulers of men. Nor will there be a time in future when any of us will cease to be. (12)

Just as the dweller of this body passes through childhood, youth and old age, so does it pass into another body. This does not confuse the wise. (13)

Contacts (of our senses) with their objects, O son of Kunti (Arjuna), give rise to the experiences of cold and heat, pleasure and pain. O Bharata (Arjuna), you must learn to bear these transient things patiently—they come and go. (14)

O the best of men (Arjuna)! The man whom these contacts do not disturb, who is even-minded in pleasure and pain, steadfast, he is fit for immortality. (15)

The unreal has no being; the real never ceases to be. The boundary between these two is thus perceived by the seers of ultimate reality. (16)

Indeed, know it to be indestructible by which all this is pervaded. No one can destroy this imperishable reality. (17)

These bodies are known to have an end; the dweller in the body (the embodied self) is eternal, imperishable and immeasurable. Therefore, O Bharata, fight! (18)

He who understands this self to be the slayer and he who takes it to be the slain, both fail to understand the truth: it does not kill nor is it killed. (19)

It is never born, nor does it ever die; nor once having been does it cease to be. Unborn, eternal, everlasting, primordial, it is not killed when the body is killed. (20)

One who knows this unborn, undying one as indestructible and everlasting, how and whom can that man, O son of Pritha, kill or cause to be killed? (21)

As a man casts off worn-out garments to put on new and different ones, so the dweller in the body (the embodied self) discards worn-out bodies to enter into others that are new. (22)

Weapons do not cut it, nor does fire burn it; waters do not wet it, nor does wind dry it. (23)

It cannot be cut or burned; it cannot be wet or yet dried; it is eternal, all-pervading, fixed, immovable, and timeless. (24)

It is declared to be unmanifest, unthinkable, and immutable. Since you know it to be so, you should not grieve. (25)

Even if you think of it as constantly being born and constantly dying, then too, O great warrior (Arjuna), you should not grieve like this. (26)

Certain is death for the born and certain is birth for the dead; therefore, this being inevitable, you should not grieve. (27)

Beings are unmanifest in the origin, manifest in the middle state and unmanifest again in the end. O Bharata! What cause of grief is there in this? (28)

One sees it as a wonder, another likewise describes it as a wonder, and as a wonder another hears of it. Yet even on seeing, speaking and hearing, rarely someone knows it. (29)

This self dwelling in the body of every being is eternal and indestructible. O Bharata, therefore you should not grieve for all these beings. (30)

Even if you consider your own *dharma* you should not waver, for there is nothing better for a kshatriya (member of the warrior caste) than a battle in accord with *dharma*. (31)

Happy are the kshatriyas, O son of Pritha, who find, unsought, such a battle—an open door to heaven. (32)

But if you fail to engage in this battle in accord with *dharma*, then abandoning your own *dharma* and fame, you will incur sin. (33)

Moreover, people will ever recount your disgrace, and to an esteemed one disgrace is worse than death. (34)

The great chariot-warriors will think you fled from battle out of fear and you will come to be held lightly by those who once held you in high esteem. (35)

And your enemies, deriding your strength, will slander you with so many unspeakable words. What, indeed, is more painful than that? (36)

Either by being killed you will gain heaven, or by winning you will enjoy earth. Therefore, O son of Kunti, stand up, resolved to fight. (37)

Treating pleasure and pain alike, gain and loss, victory and defeat, prepare yourself for the battle. Thus you will bring no evil on yourself. (38)

This understanding that has been explained to you is in terms of *Samkhya*; now hear it in terms of *yoga*. Your intellect established through this understanding, O son of Pritha, you will be released from the bondage of action. (39)

In this *yoga* no effort is lost, nor is there any adverse effect. Even a little of this *dharma* saves from great danger. (40)

O joy of the Kurus (Arjuna), in this (*yoga*) the mind is focused and resolute, but the thoughts of irresolute men are diffuse and endless. (41)

The undiscerning who are engrossed in the letter of the Veda, O son of Pritha, utter flowery speech, and declare: "There is nothing else!" (42)

Filled with desire, with heaven as their goal, they aim at the attainment and enjoyment of power; but their varied rituals yield (re)birth as the fruit of these actions. (43)

The resolute state of mind does not arise in the concentration of those who are obsessed with enjoyment and power, and whose thoughts are captivated by those flowery words. (44)

The Vedas' concern is with the three *gunas*. O Arjuna! Go beyond the three *gunas*, being free from dualities, ever firm in truth, independent of mundane rewards, established in your self. (45)

For the enlightened brahmin (member of the priest caste), all the Vedas have no more value than a small well in a place flooded with water on every side. (46)

You have claim over your actions alone and never over the fruits of action. Never live for the fruits of action nor attach yourself to inaction. (47)

O Dhananjaya (Arjuna)! Perform actions being firm in *yoga*, having abandoned attachments; be impartial to success and failure, for this equanimity is called *yoga*. (48)

O Dhananjaya! Action (done for its fruits) is far inferior to the *yoga* of understanding. So, seek refuge in understanding—wretched are those who live for the fruits of actions. (49)

Disciplined by understanding, one leaves behind both good and evil deeds in this world. Therefore, devote yourself to *yoga—yoga* is skill in actions. (50)

Wise men, disciplined by understanding, relinquish the fruits born of their actions. Being free from the bonds of rebirth, they reach a place free from all ills. (51)

When your intellect has passed beyond the thicket of delusion, you will become averse towards all that is heard and what is yet to be heard (in the Vedas). (52)

When your intellect, once bewildered (by Vedic texts), shall stand unshaken, steadfast in concentration, then you will attain *yoga*. (53)

Arjuna said:

O handsome-haired one! What is the description of a person of steadfast mind who is deep in concentration? How would such a person of steady mind speak? How would he sit? How would he move? (54)

The blessed one said:

When a man renounces all desires in his mind, O son of Pritha, when he is content in himself by the self alone, then he is said to be a person of steadfast mind. (55)

When his mind is undisturbed in the midst of sorrows, when he has no longing for pleasures, being free from passion, fear and anger, he is said to be a sage whose thought is steadfast. (56)

He who has no undue fondness towards anything, who neither rejoices nor recoils on gaining what is good or bad, his mind is firmly established. (57)

And when he is able to withdraw his senses completely from their objects, as a tortoise drawing in its limbs, his mind is firmly established. (58)

The objects of senses turn away from the embodied self who abstains from food, save for flavor. Even that too turns away when he has seen the highest (reality). (59)

O son of Kunti! The turbulent senses forcibly carry away the mind even of a discerning man who tries to control them. (60)

Having brought them all under control, let him sit controlled, intent on me; for when his senses are under control, his mind is firmly established. (61)

Dwelling on sense-objects, a man develops attachment for them; from attachment comes desire, and from desire arises anger. (62)

From anger comes delusion, from delusion come memory lapses; from memory lapses comes destruction of the intellect (the ability to think), from destruction of intellect he perishes. (63)

But one, whose senses experience sense-objects without attraction and aversion, who is self-controlled and self-restrained, he attains serenity. (64)

In serenity is born an end to all his sorrows; for the intellect of the tranquil-minded quickly becomes stable. (65)

The undisciplined has no (right) intellect, nor any sustained thought. The man without sustained thought has no peace; for one without peace how can there be joy? (66)

For, when a man's mind is governed by the wandering senses, his mind is carried away as wind carries away a ship on the water. (67)

Therefore, O great-armed warrior (Arjuna)! he whose senses are withdrawn from their objects completely, has a mind which is firmly established. (68)

What is night for all creatures, a self-controlled person is awake then; when the creatures are awake, it is night for the sage who sees (reality). (69)

As the ocean remains unmoved even when being filled by waters flowing into it, the man in whom all desires enter in that same way attains peace and not one who lusts after desires. (70)

Having relinquished all desires, when a man acts being free from longing, without possessiveness and the sense of "I" (individuality), he finds peace. (71)

This is the state of *Brahman*, O son of Pritha, and having attained it, a man is no longer confused; abiding in it even at the time of death, he attains absorption into *Brahman*. (72)

Philosopher's corner: Chapter analysis and questions for consideration

Being one of the two longest chapters of the *Gita* and one where the overview of Krishna's main argument in the rest of the *Gita* and its conceptual ingredients are introduced, this chapter offers numerous opportunities of philosophical reflection and engagements. My focus here is not to catalog all these diverse instances but to highlight a few that I find particularly interesting.

The first set of verses (namely, 2.16–27) that I find very relevant philosophically is where Krishna introduces his version of the distinction between appearance and reality: while the latter remains unchanged, the former goes through many stages and kinds of change and decay. Krishna's central point is that Arjuna's dilemma rises from a confusion (almost an equivocation) between the real that "never ceases to be" and the unreal that "has no being" (2.16). An important corollary of this distinction is the dualism that emerges—not the familiar kind of mind-body dualism of Western philosophy—but a body-self dualism. In mind-body dualism, the mind, given its essential property of consciousness, is taken to be irreducibly separate from the body, given the latter's essential property of physical extension. In body-self dualism, on the other hand, body, given its essential feature of change, is differentiated from the immutable, eternal self. In this understanding a human being (a *jiva*) is an embodied self—i.e., a self in a body—, and in virtue of having a body the self comes to have a mind and the various faculties needed to experience and act in the world. The question to explore in this regard is not only the ontology of this body-self dualism in terms of immortal selves and embodied experience, but also whether this proposed response can be entertained in other philosophical (ontological and epistemological) systems as well. Moreover, how does this distinction aim to diffuse Arjuna's dilemma? What chances are there that this counsel can really diffuse Arjuna's dilemma? For instance, in verse 2.21 Krishna says of the person who knows the truth about the everlasting self, "how and whom can that man kill or cause to be killed?" Indeed, no killing in the sense of complete destruction of a person is possible since weapons and other means of destroying the body fail to touch the self (2.23–24). However, the exact import of Krishna's counsel on the metaphysics of killing and the associated issues of morality and even legality might be an interesting location for philosophical reflection. Finally, it appears that at this moment in the text Krishna is suggesting that Arjuna's psychologically debilitating moral dilemma can be cured by his knowledge of a truth about a clear distinction. What kind of relationship between ontology, epistemology, and moral psychology does this presuppose? Indeed, Krishna's counsel offers interesting points of resonance especially in relation to recent discussions in moral psychology and on topics in philosophy of mind including attention and emotion (see, for example, Bilimoria 2004 and Johnson 2007).

Krishna argues that when our senses come in contact with their objects, such contact not only results in "the experiences of cold and heat, pleasure and pain" (2.14), but also furnishes the intentional content of these states such as to allow thinking about those objects. Such "broodings" compel the minds to develop attachment to these objects that gives rise to desire, anger, fears, and, ultimately, the "destruction of intellect" (2.62 and 63). A kind of mutuality between phenomenology and intentionality of our mental content is being suggested here. Unlike in the Western analytic tradition, where often no clear relation between phenomenology and intentionality is acknowledged, the *Gita* seems to be positing a close connection between these two. In fact, it could be argued that our first phenomenological experiences of heat and cold and others become the content of our thoughts and desires and other mental states involving them. Thus, such mutuality seems to automatically result in attachments to these contents giving rise to various emotional states of desire, anger, anguish, and fear.

Another dimension of this discussion is indicated in verse 2.39 which represents an important transition in Krishna's message. This verse articulates the transition from Samkhya to *yoga*, thereby reflecting Krishna's conviction that realization of knowledge of the eternal self depends on the preparation of the mind and intellect in terms of acquisition of certain mental virtues like steadfastness and serenity. Krishna clarifies that mind that is trained in such a way that the senses are under control becomes focused, as opposed to that of a person devoid of such cultivation (2.41). In order to control the senses,

Krishna argues, they have to be withdrawn from their objects, "as a tortoise drawing in its limbs" (2.58). It is useful to explore the moral implication of this withdrawal. Is Krishna recommending a withdrawal from our engagement with the world or only an engagement that is marked by an attachment to the world? The *Gita*, of course, argues that it is the latter but it is productive to explore the exact nature of an engagement with the world that is without attachment. Also relevant in this context is the role of experience like pleasure, pain, peace, and joy in Krishna's counsel. While, according to Krishna, one must learn to "bear the transient things" like pleasure and pain patiently (2.14), one should aspire for serenity (2.65), and peace and joy (2.66). What might be the implication of this distinction for a theory of emotions?

In the Introduction I pointed out that though it is generally maintained that the *Gita* discusses three *yoga*s, namely, that of action, knowledge, and devotion, another *yoga*—the *yoga* of understanding (*buddhi yoga*)—is also emphasized in the *Gita*. Nowhere is this more evident than in the set of verses 49–53 of the present chapter. Krishna encourages Arjuna to commit to *buddhi yoga* or the *yoga* of understanding (2.49) such that his intellect is able to stand "unshaken, steadfast in concentration" (2.53) and is not bewildered by the Vedic texts or their various injunctions. Given this characterization, it could be argued that while the *yoga* of knowledge is marked by meditations on the self thereby a cultivation of the mind, the *yoga* of understanding is marked by a cultivation of the intellect and rationality (see also Phillips 2009, 178–179).

The final set of verses that interests me from this chapter deals with the range of meanings in which the term *dharma* is employed in this chapter. In his opening remarks Arjuna confesses his confusion about his *dharma*. Krishna's response reflects a multidimensional understanding of *dharma*. While verse 2.33 argues that Arjuna should fight because this battle is "in accord with [his caste] *dharma*," verse 2.40 articulates *dharma* in terms of *karma yoga* or having attained equanimity in one's attitude. *Dharma* is often rendered as "duty" when it is translated into English and as a result in the context of comparative philosophy it is understood purely in its moral dimension. However, what this set of verses allows us to appreciate is the multiple dimensionalities of *dharma* and their relevance to our moral deliberations. The idea of equanimity as a central aspect of the ethics of *yoga* also draws our attention to an emergent characteristic of *Gita*'s ethical theory: if we understand equanimity as going beyond the pairs of opposites of physical and psychological dualities, then the goal of the *Gita* seems to be to realize a kind of trans-morality where agency ultimately fades away. How actionable might this trans-morality be?

3

The Yoga of Action

Summary

This chapter introduces one of the most important concepts of the *Gita*, namely, the *yoga* of action. Chapter 2 concluded with Krishna articulating in detail the characteristics of a person whose mind is firmly established in *yoga*. Virtues like self-control, serenity, and relinquishment of desires were highlighted. Arjuna's opening question in Chapter 3 assumes that these virtues are inherently cultivated through knowledge and thus asks, if that is the case then why is Krishna asking him to engage in the "violent action" of killing his near and dear ones? In response Krishna clarifies the nature of the *yoga* of action. More specifically he outlines the source of action, and considers the viability of actionlessness, and the relation between action and attachment, and between agency and individuality. In this process the grammar of selfless or non-selfish action, i.e., action done as pure sacrifice or action performed without attachment, is explained. Krishna also emphasizes that virtues like self-control and relinquishment of desire are essential aspects of attitudes that promote self-realization and thereby enable selfless action.

Arjuna said:

O Janardana! If you consider knowledge to be superior to action, then O handsome-haired one, why do you enjoin me to this violent action? (1)

These apparently opposed statements of yours are confusing my understanding. So tell me the one definitive truth by which I may achieve the best. (2)

The blessed one (Krishna) said:

O blameless one (Arjuna)! Earlier I taught that there are two paths in this world: the *yoga* of knowledge of the followers of discrimination (i.e., philosophers) and the *yoga* of action of the followers of action. (3)

A man does not attain actionlessness by abstaining from action; nor does he attain perfection by mere renunciation. (4)

No one, indeed, can exist even for a moment without performing action; for everyone is helplessly made to act by the *gunas* born of Prakriti. (5)

Restraining the organs of actions, one who sits dwelling on the sense-objects in his mind; he is said to be a self-deluded hypocrite. (6)

But he, who, controlling the senses by the mind, engages the organs of action in the *yoga* of action without attachment, excels, O Arjuna! (7)

Perform your required duties for action is better than inaction; even the maintenance of your own body is not possible without action. (8)

People are bound by action unless it is done as sacrifice; O son of Kunti (Arjuna)! Perform action for that purpose, being freed from attachment. (9)

In the beginning, after creating living beings along with sacrifice, Prajapati, the primordial creator, said: "By sacrifice you will procreate and let this (sacrifice) be the wish-granting cow[1] that brings you fulfillment of your desires." (10)

Nourish the gods with this sacrifice so that those gods may nourish you; by sustaining one another, you will attain the highest good. (11)

Nourished by sacrifice, the gods will certainly give you the delights you desire. But he who enjoys their gifts without giving to them in return, is merely a thief. (12)

The righteous, who eat the remnants of sacrifice, are freed from all sins; but the unrighteous, who prepare food for themselves alone, eat the food of sin. (13)

Creatures come into being from food, food arises from rain; rain comes from sacrifice, sacrifice originates in action. (14)

Know that action arises from *Brahman*, while *Brahman* springs from the imperishable. Therefore, the all-pervading *Brahman* is ever established in sacrifice. (15)

O son of Pritha (Arjuna)! He who does not follow in this world the wheel thus set revolving is sinful; delighting in the senses, he lives in vain. (16)

But the man who finds delight in the self alone, and is satisfied in the self; who finds contentment only in the self, for him there is nothing more to be done. (17)

Neither has he any profit to gain in this life from the actions he has done or from the actions he has not done, nor does his purpose depend on any other creature. (18)

Therefore, always perform any action that must be done without attachment. For by performing action without attachment a person achieves the highest. (19)

Janaka and others attained perfection by action alone. Moreover, recognizing (its need) even for the welfare of the world you must perform action. (20)

Whatever a great man does, the very same is also done by others; whatever standard he sets, the world follows it. (21)

There is no action in the three worlds that I must do, O son of Pritha! Nor is there anything left to be attained, and yet I still continue in action. (22)

For if I did not always engage in action ceaselessly, O son of Pritha, men would follow my path at every turn. (23)

These worlds would collapse if I did not perform action; I would be the agent of confusion (in society) and would destroy these beings. (24)

As the ignorant act with attachment to action, O Bharata (Arjuna), so the wise should act, but without any attachment, for the welfare of the world. (25)

Let the wise man not cause confusion in the minds of ignorant men who are attached to action. By acting with discipline, let the wise bring them to enjoy all actions. (26)

Actions are in every case performed by the *gunas* of Prakriti; but he whose mind is deluded by the sense of "I" (individuality) thinks, "I am the agent." (27)

But O mighty-armed (Arjuna), he, who knows the truth about the separation (of the self) from both the *gunas* and their actions, knowing that *gunas* act on (other) *gunas*, remains unattached. (28)

Those deluded by the *gunas* of Prakriti are attached to their actions; a man of perfect knowledge should not disturb these dull men of imperfect knowledge. (29)

Surrendering all actions to me and focusing your mind on the supreme self; freed from longing and possessiveness, delivered from the fever (of delusion), fight the battle! (30)

Those who constantly follow this doctrine of mine, trusting it without complaining, are also liberated from (the bondage of) action. (31)

But those who find fault and do not follow my doctrine, know them to be deluded about all knowledge, doomed and mindless. (32)

Even a wise person acts in accordance with his own nature; creatures follow their own nature, what will restraint accomplish? (33)

Attraction and hatred of each sense are located in the object of that sense experience; one must not come under control of these two for both indeed are enemies lurking on his path! (34)

One's own *dharma*, done imperfectly, is better than performing another's *dharma* well; better to die in one's own *dharma* for another's *dharma* is perilous. (35)

Arjuna said:

Then what impels a person to commit sin, even involuntarily, as if compelled by force, O varshneya? (36)

The blessed one said:

It is desire, it is anger, arising from the *guna* of passion—all-consuming and most sinful. Know it as the enemy here (on earth). (37)

As fire is obscured by smoke and a mirror by dirt; as an embryo is covered by its caul, so is this (knowledge) obscured by (desire and anger). (38)

Knowledge is obscured by this constant enemy of the wise man, which takes the form of desire and is an insatiable fire, O son of Kunti. (39)

The senses, mind, and understanding are said to be its (desire's) seat; having obscured knowledge with these it deludes the dweller in the body (embodied self). (40)

Therefore, O bull of the Bharatas (Arjuna), having first restrained your senses, kill this sinful (desire), the destroyer of theoretical and practical knowledge. (41)

The senses, they say, are superior (to their objects); higher than the senses is the mind; but higher than the mind is the intellect, while higher than the intellect is He (the self). (42)

Thus, knowing that which is higher than the intellect, sustaining the self with the self, O mighty-armed, kill the enemy in the form of desire that is difficult to subdue. (43)

Philosopher's corner: Chapter analysis and questions for consideration

The opening theme of this chapter is that actionlessness—understood in terms of abstention from action—is neither an attainable nor a desirable goal. Actionlessness is not attainable since no one can abstain from performing action even for an instance (3.5). It thus becomes akin to the concept of a frictionless plane of physics, as the very nature of our reality, as constituted by Prakriti and its *gunas*, necessitates constant change and transformation. We, being partially constituted of the *gunas*, cannot escape action. Further, all action performed with the intention of fulfilling some desire(s) binds—imprisons—the performer to future action (3.9; see also 3.33). Krishna's argument here draws from the theory of karma that argues that all intentional action performed for a desired outcome produces a residue that the agent of the action has to face later. Actionlessness is not desirable either since even the maintenance of our own bodies is not possible without action (3.8). Further, if one stops engaging with the sense-objects while constantly "dwelling on the sense objects in the mind" then the goal of self-control remains illusory for such "a self-deluded hypocrite" (3.6). So the important question is not whether, but *how* one should engage in action. The *yoga* of action requires one to perform action "without attachment" (3.7) to the expected outcome of an action (3.25). Such an action constitutes sacrifice—or actions performed not for specific outcomes but simply as duty. In fact, in characterizing sacrifice as an offering to the gods, Krishna here highlights the inner dimension of sacrifice where acts of sacrifice become gifts of love to the Divine.[2] Such action allows one to "find delight in the self alone"—and satisfaction and contentment as well—and no purpose or goal remains to be attained for such a person. Thus, we can be free from being attached to our actions. What enables us such non-attachment is knowledge of the true nature of self and its distinction from the *gunas*.

Another central theme of this chapter is the dualism between the self, and the Prakriti and the *gunas* that constitute it (3.28). This chapter thus further elaborates the body-self dualism introduced in Chapter 2. This dualism is important because a clear understanding of this distinction turns out to be essential to one's ability to perform "unattached action." Ignorance of this distinction results in a misconception about the location of agency. Attachment to action results when one takes the self to be the agent and not the *gunas* or the Prakriti. Krishna analyzes attachment in terms of ownership: "Actions are in every case performed by the *gunas* of Prakriti; but he whose mind is deluded by the sense of 'I' (individuality) thinks, 'I am the actor'" (3.27). Here Krishna not only delineates the mechanism of action but also exposes that attachment lies at the core of our sense of agency. Taking the self to be the agent, and not the *gunas* where desires and various emotions including anger reside, a person—ignorant of this distinction—attaches all his faculties to sense-objects. Action without attachment requires that one control one's senses by refraining from this false sense of agency. The resultant knowledge of the nature of the self allows one to act without attachment; acting from that discernment is the sole way to attain self-realization. Indeed, this dualism allows us to clarify the meaning of Krishna's claim that a person who performs action without attachment "delights in the self alone" is "satisfied in the self," and finds "contentment only in the self" (3.17). If not viewed in the context of this dualism, this verse (3.17) might be taken as permission for self-centered self-absorption. However, the self that is referred to in this context is not the embodied individuality that we commonly associate with our understanding of the self. Rather, the self that is implied here is the eternal and unchanging self that forms the core of every animate existence, and freedom and self-realization come from knowing its true nature.

Krishna's recommendation of action without attachment (3.19) has been readily compared with the Kantian notion of the categorical imperative of duty for duty's sake. Given the emphasis that the categorical imperative puts on impartiality understood in terms of transcending individuating factors including desires and other emotions, the similarity between the two is important to note. However, a careful reading of Chapter 3 also allows us to appreciate a few interesting differences. First, here Krishna does not seem to abide by the pure formalism of the categorical imperative. One of the markers of the categorical imperative, according to Kant, is its universalizability, i.e., the fact that *everyone* can and should act with the same maxim or motive. There is no similar universalizability required of action without attachment in the *Gita*. Thus, in characterizing action without attachment as sacrifice Krishna not only includes the various acts of sacrifice prescribed in the Vedic texts, but also expands the reference to include his own action (3.22, 3.24) as well as action "for the welfare of the world" (3.25). Further, the categorical imperative, given its emphasis on impartiality, is not able to accommodate Krishna's suggestion to "sustain the self with the self" (3.43), whereas, the dualism of self and Prakriti that informs Krishna's characterization of sacrifice allows for a more nuanced understanding of agency. Finally, Krishna considers desire to be the enemy of self (3.43) in a way that Kant does not and need not. Granted that desires that cannot be universalized are not accepted within the scope of the categorical imperative. However, that does not imply that *all* desires are to be excluded or that are to be conquered through the controlling of the senses (3.41). Indeed, a careful exploration of the scope of comparison between the *yoga* of action and Kant's categorical imperative is a worthwhile question to pursue.[3]

Notes

1 Hindu mythological figure with "a woman's head, a cow's body and a bird's wings" (Chidbhavananda 1997, 225).

2 This point would be further developed in the subsequent chapters of the *Gita* especially while outlining the *yoga* of devotion. It also shows that the *yoga* of action includes an element of devotion or bhakti. I thank Stephen Phillips for helping me see this point.

3 See Maitra 2006 for more on the comparison between the *Gita* and Kant.

4

The Yoga of Renunciation of Action through Knowledge

Summary

This chapter develops further aspects of the *yoga* of action by delineating Krishna's role in the propagation of its teaching. Krishna describes himself as the teacher of this *yoga* who transmits it through the ages. This thus sets the stage for him to reveal his incarnated nature later in the chapter. The chapter also offers two additional elucidations of this *yoga*: Krishna presents himself as an exemplar of action without attachment; he also explains the nature of action by clarifying the distinction between action, inaction, and wrong action. While wrong action involves action motivated by selfish desire and attachment, and inaction involves attempted refrain from action due to ignorance about the nature of self and reality, action is understood as undertakings free from desires and thoughts of incentives. It is this last category that the *yoga* of action recommends. After cataloging various kinds of sacrifice, Krishna recognizes the sacrifice of knowledge as the highest kind given its purifying power. He thus emphasizes the role of knowledge in the renunciation of action by clarifying that sacrifice that is of the nature of pure offering is at the heart of action of a "non-doer."

The blessed one (Krishna) said:
I taught this undying *yoga* to Vivasvat (the brilliant sun); Vivasvat taught it to Manu (the progenitor of humanity); Manu declared it to Ikshvaku (the solar king, son of Manu). (1)

The royal sages knew this *yoga* having received it from the tradition. But over the long lapse of time in this world, O scorcher of foes (Arjuna), it became lost. (2)

This is the same ancient *yoga* that I have taught to you today because you are my devotee and my friend. For this is a supreme secret. (3)

Arjuna said:
Later is your birth (whereas) earlier is the birth of Vivasvat, the sun; how may I comprehend this that you declared it in the beginning? (4)

The blessed one said:
Many (past) births of mine have passed away and of yours too, O Arjuna. I know them all but you do not, O scorcher of foes! (5)

Although I am unborn, although my self is imperishable, although I am lord of beings, yet taking on my phenomenal form, I come into being by my own *maya*. (6)

For whenever *dharma* decays and *adharma* flourishes, O Bharata (Arjuna), then I send myself forth. (7)

For the protection of the righteous and for the destruction of evil-doers, in order to firmly establish *dharma*, I come into being age after age. (8)

One who thus truly knows my divine birth and action does not undergo rebirth on leaving the body; he comes to me, O Arjuna. (9)

Freed from passion, fear and anger, absorbed in me, taking refuge in me, purified by the austerity of knowledge, many have come to my being. (10)

In whatever way anyone approaches me, I grant them favor in that very manner; in every way, O son of Pritha (Arjuna), human beings follow my path. (11)

Those who desire success in their actions here on earth make (sacrificial) offering to the gods, for success born of such action comes quickly in the human world. (12)

The fourfold order (classes) was created by me according to the division of *gunas* and actions. Though I am its author, know me as the immutable non-doer. (13)

Actions do not defile me (for) I have no yearning for their fruits; one who knows me thus is not bound by actions. (14)

Knowing this, even the ancient seekers of liberation performed actions; therefore, you simply perform action as they did in the ancient times. (15)

What is action? What is inaction? About this even the seer-poets are perplexed; therefore, I will explain action to you, knowing that you will be freed from evil. (16)

For one must understand (the nature of) action, must understand (the nature of) wrong action, and must understand (the nature of) inaction as well; inscrutable is the way of action. (17)

One who sees action in inaction and inaction in action, he is wise among men; disciplined in *yoga*, he does all action. (18)

One, whose every undertaking is free from desire and the incentives thereof, whose actions are burnt up in the fire of knowledge, is called learned by the wise. (19)

Having abandoned attachment to the fruits of action, being always content, independent, he does nothing at all even when engaged in action. (20)

Expecting nothing, his mind and self controlled, relinquishing all possessions, performing actions with the body alone, he incurs no sin. (21)

Content with whatever comes to him by chance, transcending the dualities, free from envy, even-minded in success and failure; even acting he is not bound. (22)

The actions of a person who is unattached and free, whose mind is established in knowledge, who acts only as sacrifice, are wholly dissolved. (23)

Brahman is the act of offering; *Brahman* is the oblation poured by *Brahman* into (ritual) fire that is *Brahman*; to *Brahman* alone must one who places their actions in *Brahman* go. (24)

Some yogis (men of *yoga*) perform sacrifice merely by worshipping the gods, others by offering the sacrifice itself into the fire that is *Brahman*. (25)

Some offer hearing and other senses in the fires of restraint; others offer sound and other sense-objects in the fires of the senses. (26)

Others offer all actions of the senses and all actions of breath in the fire of *yoga* kindled by knowledge—which is self-control. (27)

Some perform sacrifice by means of material objects, by austerity or by the practice of *yoga*; while other ascetics of rigid vows offer their scriptural learning and knowledge as their sacrifice. (28)

Others again, who are devoted to breathing exercises, sacrifice by pouring the inward into the outward breath and the outward into the inward, having restrained the flow of inhalation and exhalation. (29)

Yet others, restricting their food, sacrifice by offering their life-breaths into life-breaths; all these indeed understand sacrifice and through sacrifice their sins are destroyed. (30)

O best of Kurus (Arjuna)! Men who eat the nectar of the remnants of sacrifice reach the eternal *Brahman*. This world is not for him who offers no sacrifice; how then the next? (31)

In this way sacrifices of many kinds are set forth in the face of *Brahman*; know that they all are born of action and thus knowing you will find release. (32)

Sacrifice of knowledge is better than sacrifice with material objects, O scorcher of foes; all actions, without exception, culminate completely in knowledge, O son of Pritha! (33)

Know this by humble submission (to those who can teach it), by questioning and by serving (them), (for) the wise, who have experienced reality, will instruct you in this knowledge. (34)

Knowing which, O son of Pandu (Arjuna), you will not fall into this delusion again; for through this knowledge you will see all beings, without exception, in your self and also in me. (35)

Even if you are the most sinful of all sinners, you will cross over all evil by the boat of knowledge alone. (36)

As a kindled fire reduces fuel to ashes, O Arjuna, so the fire of knowledge turns all actions into ashes. (37)

Truly there is nothing in this world so purifying as knowledge; in time the person of perfect *yoga* finds this in his own self. (38)

He, who is faithful, devoted (to knowledge) and has restrained his senses, gains knowledge; having gained knowledge he soon achieves supreme peace. (39)

The ignorant man, who is faithless and filled with self-doubt, perishes; for the doubting mind has no happiness—either in this world or in the next. (40)

One, whose actions are renounced by *yoga*, who has dispelled doubt with knowledge, who is in possession of himself, is not bound by action, O Dhananjaya (Arjuna)! (41)

So sever this doubt in your heart born out of ignorance with the sword of self-knowledge, and be established in *yoga*. Rise, O Bharata! (42)

Philosopher's corner: Chapter analysis and questions for consideration

The chapter opens with a restatement of the Hindu theme, shared with Buddhist and Jain perspectives, of rebirth—the idea that some aspect of every being goes through different births. Krishna reiterates that both Arjuna and he have been through many births (4.5). The distinction between rebirth and reincarnation is also drawn with the fact that only in the latter case—in the case of Vishnu/Krishna assuming the human form of Krishna—one remembers the previous multiple births. The role of memory in drawing this distinction and the underlying mechanism might be an interesting question to explore. Additionally Krishna elaborates why and how he comes to assume a human form: "for the protection of the righteous and for the destruction of evil-doers" (4.8) he comes into being through the power of his "own *maya*" (4.6) that he will identify in a later chapter (see, for example, 7.14) as his lower nature. So Krishna is definitely adding another premise to his overall argument of why Arjuna must fight, namely, that given the prevailing *adharma* of the Kauravas (Arjuna's cousins and opponents in the battle), Krishna has assumed a human form and by joining the fight Arjuna will be part of his plan. This provides a more concrete anchor for Krishna's main premise so far championed, which is that Arjuna's worry is based on a fundamental misunderstanding of the nature of self, action, and agency. The interesting question to ask in this regard is whether the nature of Krishna's main argument changes as a result of this addition.

While the verses 7 and 8 are often used as evidence for Vishnu appearing in the human form of Krishna, it is important to note, following Deutsch, that such a straight forward rendition is "inconsistent with the rest of the teaching about the nature of the divine and the world which is put forward by the *Gita*" (1968, 18). The specific points of contention are the claims that Krishna makes in the *Gita*, namely, that Prakriti is *his* lower nature and (later on in 7.6) that he is the origin of the whole world and also its dissolution. Thus the inconsistency seems obvious: As Deutsch writes, "it would certainly be odd if the Lord were to enter into his own lower nature whenever it goes astray—this lower nature, which is controlled by Him, is an illusion when seen as separate from Him, and is destined to dissolve—in order to adjust it for the benefit of those living beings whose primary duty is precisely to overcome all attachment to it!" (Deutsch 1968, 19). Deutsch wants us to look at possibly an "allegorical" resolution of the avatara theme in the *Gita*. Whether one is convinced by the Deutsch resolution, it is a good topic for further exploration.

The gift of this chapter for philosophers is verse 18 which identifies a wise person as one who "sees action in inaction and inaction in action." What does it mean to see the juxtaposition of action in inaction and inaction in action? Here Krishna draws from the metaphysical distinction that confines action entirely to the realm of Prakriti, which is the location of change, and differentiates it from the true self that remains untouched by the changes. Being unaware of this distinction, if one identifies oneself with one's mind then even in not engaging in physical actions one might create further bondage by the mental act of such identification. Hence follows action in inaction. On the contrary, if one is acting from true understanding of the locus of all actions, then since even in action one is not causing bondage for the self, that action remains inaction. According to Krishna such a person "does nothing at all even when engaged in action" (4.20). A further presupposition is the karma theory that maintains that every intentional action performed out of attachment produces a residue that binds the self. But is there a way of articulating this juxtaposition of action and inaction if we don't assume the metaphysical confusion between Prakriti and the true self? Is this similar to the Daoist idea of *wu wei*? Is this the same as the Kantian dictum of impartiality? These comparative contexts will offer opportunities to better understand the dynamics between action and inaction.

One of the main themes of this chapter is the role of knowledge in renunciation of action. As Krishna develops this theme, such renunciation ultimately becomes locations of inner sacrifice where actions become mere offerings to *Brahman* or Krishna. After considering a range of different kinds of sacrifices involving material objects or breathing exercises or the restriction of food (4.24–31), Krishna clarifies that sacrifice of knowledge is the highest form of sacrifice. Knowledge here is of the true nature of self and its distinction from Prakriti. When our sacrifice is illuminated by this knowledge, then our actions become pure offerings since all other intentions or motivations involving desired outcome become "burnt up in the fire of knowledge" (4.19; see also 4.37). Such pure offerings result in renunciation or inaction even in action since action coupled with this realization is "wholly dissolved" (4.23) as not causing any further bondage (4.22). Krishna concludes that a person who has renounced his actions, whose actions have become pure offerings, whose doubts have been dispelled by knowledge of his true nature, is a person whose actions don't bind him (4.41). Of course this leaves us with a lingering question: since no performance of action of pure offering, of renunciation, is possible until one has gained the knowledge of the true nature of self, then doesn't the *yoga* of action become dependent on and arguably subsumed under the *yoga* of knowledge?

Finally exploring the exact nature of knowledge that Krishna claims to be liberating, by which one "achieves supreme peace" (4.39), is rewarding from a philosophical perspective. While the exact mechanism of this knowledge has not been articulated yet, it is clear that the quest for this knowledge does not start with a doubt or even a question. Indeed, skeptics, those who are "filled with self-doubt," have no happiness either in this world or the next according to the *Gita* (4.40). Further this knowledge with transformative power—liberating the most sinful of all sinners (4.36)—requires one's faithful devotion (4.39) and humble submission (4.34). The emphasis, therefore, is on the manner of knowing along with the content of knowledge.

5

The Yoga of Renunciation

Summary

Arjuna opens this chapter with a question implied by Krishna's counsel in Chapter 4, namely, which is preferable—the performance of action or the renunciation of action? While Krishna responds initially that the *yoga* of action is "superior to the renunciation of action"—presumably because renunciation is harder and moreover renunciation is "hard to attain" without the *yoga* of action—but he clarifies quickly that there is no difference of any importance between the two as they both produce the same result: the highest good that is "eternal happiness" or "eternal freedom." Drawing on the nature of agency that Krishna began developing in Chapter 4, he adds here that in every undertaking a yogi performs action with the body, mind, intellect, and the senses—the *only* viable location of agency—without ever attaching to the outcomes of the action. He clarifies that this produces lasting peace through fostering equanimity, or the ability of equal vision, whereby one is able to see disparate things as same as oneself. Krishna concludes the chapter with an account on the nature of equanimity and its cognitive, moral, and social dimensions.

Arjuna said:

O Krishna! You praise renunciation of action and again *yoga* (of action); tell me definitively which one is the better of these two. (1)

The blessed one (Krishna) said:

Both renunciation of action and the *yoga* of action lead to the highest good; but, of the two, the *yoga* of action is superior to the renunciation of action. (2)

One who neither hates nor craves is to be recognized as a man of constant renunciation; for being free from the pairs of opposites, he is easily freed from bondage, O mighty-armed (Arjuna)! (3)

Simpletons, and not the learned, pronounce *Samkhya* and *yoga* (of action) to be separate; for one who is established firmly in one attains the fruit of both. (4)

The place attained by the philosophers is also reached by the yogis (men of *yoga*); he truly sees who sees that *Samkhya* and *yoga* (of action) are one. (5)

But renunciation is hard to attain without *yoga* (of action), O mighty-armed; the sage intent on *yoga* goes to *Brahman* without delay. (6)

Disciplined in *yoga*, with purified self, he, who has fully mastered himself and has conquered his senses, whose self has become (one with) the self of all beings, is not tainted even when he acts. (7)

In seeing, hearing, touching, smelling, eating, walking, sleeping, breathing a yogi who knows the truth should think: "I am doing nothing at all;" (8)

In speaking, giving, taking and even in opening and closing of the eyes, he holds simply: "it is (only) the senses that engage in sense-objects." (9)

He who acts, placing all his actions in *Brahman*, abandoning attachment, is not tainted by sin, as a lotus leaf (is unstained) by water. (10)

Abandoning attachment, yogis perform action only with the body, mind, intellect and also the senses for self-purification. (11)

Having abandoned the fruit of action, a yogi attains lasting peace; a man who is not disciplined in *yoga* is bound being attached to the fruit of his actions due to desire. (12)

Renouncing all actions with the mind, the embodied self in control rests happily in its city of nine gates—it neither acts nor causes actions to be done. (13)

The lord of the world creates neither the agency of actions nor the actions of beings; nor does he create the link between actions and their fruits; but inherent nature initiates these. (14)

The lord (the all-pervading intelligence) does not take on the sins or good deeds of any one; knowledge is obscured by ignorance, whereby creatures are deluded. (15)

But for whom that ignorance is destroyed by the knowledge of the self, their knowledge illumines that supreme (reality) like the sun. (16)

Comprehending that, their self focused on that, being supremely devoted to that, with that being their final goal, they go to a state of beyond return, having their sins destroyed by knowledge. (17)

Wise men see the same thing in a scholarly and humble brahmin (member of the priest caste), a cow, an elephant, even a dog and an outcaste. (18)

Even here in this life those who have their minds established in equanimity have conquered rebirth, for flawless is *Brahman* and equally present everywhere; therefore, they are established in *Brahman*. (19)

One whose understanding is secure, who is undeluded, who will neither rejoice in obtaining what is dear to him, nor grieve in obtaining what is unpleasant, in knowing the *Brahman*, he abides in it. (20)

One whose self is detached from external contacts, who finds that happiness which is in the self; who is joined in *yoga* with *Brahman*, he attains eternal happiness. (21)

For all pleasures born of contact (with external objects) are only sources of sorrow, (and) have a beginning and an end, O son of Kunti (Arjuna); no wise man rejoices in them. (22)

One, who is able, even here, before being liberated from the body, to endure the impulse born of desire and anger, who is disciplined (in *yoga*); he is the happy man. (23)

One whose happiness is within, whose contentment is within, similarly whose illumination is only within, that yogi, becoming one with *Brahman*, attains eternal freedom in *Brahman*. (24)

With their sins destroyed, their dualities (doubts) dispelled, their selves controlled, seers, rejoicing in the good of all creatures, attain eternal freedom in *Brahman*. (25)

To the ascetics, who are free from desire and anger, who have controlled their mind and who have realized the self, the eternal freedom in *Brahman* is near. (26)

Shutting out external contacts, and fixing the gaze between the eyebrows, having balanced the ingoing and outgoing breaths as they flow through the nose; (27)

Controlling the senses, mind, and intellect, the sage, who is intent on liberation and whose desire, fear, and anger have ceased, is indeed truly freed. (28)

Knowing me as the enjoyer of sacrifices and austerities, great lord of the whole world, as the friend of all beings, he attains peace. (29)

Philosopher's corner: Chapter analysis and questions for consideration

The contrast between action and renunciation that forms the focus of this chapter also implies the contrast between action and knowledge since, as Krishna explained in Chapter 4, no genuine renunciation is possible without the knowledge of true self. Krishna's response here thus has bearing on one of the important internal debates within the Hindu philosophy and ethics as to the relative merits of the *yoga* of action and the *yoga* of knowledge. While the *Gita* in general emphasizes the *yoga* of action, here Krishna also wants to diffuse the perceived tension between action and knowledge. As he explains, only simpletons make this distinction between philosophy and action (5.4), between theory and practice. The plausibility of Krishna's argument here depends on his analysis of the *yoga* of action in terms of action without attachment, or action performed without the hope of a desired outcome and action performed as pure offering. According to the argument Krishna has developed so far, *yoga* of action is not possible as long as the sense of agency prevails and in order to overcome the sense of agency one requires the knowledge of self. As Krishna says, "knowledge is obscured by ignorance, whereby creatures are deluded" (5.15) and thus perform action from desire. So an intricate relation between action and knowledge seems to follow in this metaphysical framework. But it will be interesting to explore the relevance of this argument for the age-old tension between theory and practice, between knowing what ought to be done and doing what ought to be done, in the context of Western ethics.

Krishna also further develops his analysis of the ethics of action without attachment. Verses 11 and 12 elaborate the mechanics of this kind of action by explaining that the "body, mind, intellect and also the senses" are engaged in this kind of action for the purification of the self and not for the "fruit of action." Here Krishna seems to be giving us a far more nuanced sense of the mechanics than what is often offered in Western deontological ethics given its focus on reason. Part of the reason for the robustness of Krishna's response might originate in the synthetic or organic nature of Hindu philosophy where, unlike in the Western tradition, the clear compartmentalization between metaphysics, ethics, and epistemology or between mind and body does not happen.

There is another important element of philosophical interest in Krishna's counsel here as the virtue of knowledge seems to come to the forefront. In prioritizing the *yoga* of action over *yoga* of renunciation or knowledge, it appears that he is arguing that this kind of knowledge follows action not only in the result it produces but also in the preparation that it requires. Thus knowledge no longer remains a pure case of having working faculties under normal conditions; but it does not result from pure grace either. It is clearly implied to be an achievement requiring disciplined preparation and prolonged effort.

The ethics of action without attachment identifies the typical positive ideals of peace, happiness, and contentment as goals. Krishna clarifies that peace comes from a happiness that is within and a contentment that is also within (5.24; see also 5.29). However, this results not from self-centeredness, but instead from a realization of sameness of every being, or what has been called the virtue of equanimity. Equanimity has been identified by some of the philosophers of the *Gita* as the most fundamental virtue that the text proposes. Equanimity in its ethical dimension is understood as the ability to remain unaffected by gaining pleasurable *or* painful things or the ability to remain unperturbed in moments of satisfaction *and* frustration of desires (5.20). What underlines this ability is the cognitive dimension of equanimity, which means the ability to see everything as the same. Conversely, it also implies the ability to see widely disparate and even contrasting things—a Brahmin and an outcaste, a cow and a dog, for example—to be the same (5.18). What enables this internal transformation is the knowledge of the true nature of the self or *Brahman* (5.19). The *Gita's* signature contribution to this discussion is the social dimension of equanimity that it outlines. In this dimension a person with equanimity not only sees everything—pleasant as well as unpleasant things, and the immense diversity of the world—as the same but also "rejoices in the good of all creatures" (5.25). This thus makes "eternal freedom" possible. The *Gita* treats these three above dimensions, namely, the ethical and the cognitive on the one hand and the social on the other, as different sides of the same coin. But the question still remains whether equanimity implies these three dimensions as a matter of metaphysical necessity. Further, a good question to ask is how the ability to remain unperturbed in the face of changing personal fortune might also result in seeing the world through a lens of equality and also rejoicing in the good of all creatures. While one might argue that the first ability is implied by certain versions of Stoicism, the second or third ability does not necessarily and directly follow in Stoicism.

6

The Yoga of Meditation

Summary

Even though this chapter is titled "The Yoga of Meditation," we don't get a direct definition of meditation. Instead Krishna lays out how meditation is foundational for the other *yoga*s he has developed so far in the *Gita*, namely, that of action, knowledge, and renunciation. One who devotes oneself to the *yoga* of meditation—one who has "ascended to the *yoga*" of meditation—is considered a "yogi." A yogi "raises the self by the self," conquers her "self through that very self," and, further, does not "degrade the self." As a result the yogi's mind becomes one-pointed, tranquil, and all its passions are calmed through the practice of meditation. This chapter thus develops a philosophy of meditation, not only in terms of what it accomplishes or how it should be practiced, but also in terms of articulating its underlying ontology given the state of the yogi's mind, sense of self and relation to the unity of reality. Krishna outlines the role of moderation in the practice of meditation and further develops the notion of equanimity in terms of even temperament. Arjuna also gets Krishna to acknowledge the immense difficulty involved in the practice of meditation since human mind is "unsteady," "impetuous, strong, and stubborn" by nature, and very difficult—if not impossible—to control. Krishna reassures that no attempt at meditation is wasted and as a result seems to imply that the process is as important as the final result of infinite joy in the practice of meditation.

The blessed one (Krishna) said:

One, who performs actions that are required (by the scriptures) without depending on the fruit of action, is a renouncer and a yogi; not one who maintains no ritual fires and performs no rites. (1)

Know that to be the *yoga* what men call renunciation, O son of Pandu (Arjuna), for no one becomes a yogi without relinquishing purpose. (2)

Action is said to be the means for a sage desirous of ascending to *yoga*; for the man who has ascended to *yoga*, tranquility is said to be the means. (3)

For when a man does not cling to sense objects and to actions, when he has relinquished all purpose, then he is said to have ascended to *yoga*. (4)

One should raise the self by the self, one should not degrade the self; for indeed the self alone is the self's friend and the self alone is the self's enemy. (5)

The self is the friend of one who conquers his self through that very self; but for one who has not conquered his self, his self behaves with enmity like a foe. (6)

For a man who has conquered his self and who is tranquil, his transcendent self remains constant, in cold and heat, in pleasure and pain, and in honor and disgrace. (7)

That yogi, whose self is content with knowledge and realization, who has mastered his senses, who remains unshaken, (and) to whom clods, stones, and gold are the same, is said to be disciplined (in *yoga*). (8)

He excels who has even temperament toward well-wishers, friends, and foes, toward neutrals and impartials, toward those who are hateful, toward relatives, and even toward good as well as evil men. (9)

Let the yogi constantly discipline himself, remaining in a secret place, alone; his self and thoughts controlled, free from desires, (and) without possessions. (10)

Having established for himself a steady seat in a clean place, neither too high nor too low, after placing sacred grass, deerskin and cloth one upon the other; (11)

Having made his mind one-pointed, restraining the activity of his thought and senses, let him practice *yoga* for self-purification while sitting on that seat. (12)

Holding his body, head, and neck erect, motionless and steady; gazing at the tip of his nose without looking in any (other) direction, (13)

With his self tranquil, free from fear, firm in the vow of chastity, his mind controlled, let him sit disciplined in *yoga* with his thoughts focused on me, devoted to me. (14)

Ever thus collecting himself, the yogi with his mind controlled attains peace, the supreme freedom that exists in me. (15)

But, O Arjuna! *yoga* is not for him who eats too much or for him who starves himself; nor is it for him who sleeps excessively or yet for him who is (excessively) wakeful. (16)

For him who is moderate in food and recreation, who moderates his efforts in action, and who is moderate in sleep and waking this *yoga* destroys sorrow. (17)

When his controlled mind rests within the self alone, free from craving for all (objects of) desires, then he is said to be disciplined (in *yoga*). (18)

"Like a lamp which does not flicker [when placed] in a windless place" is the simile given for a yogi—controlled in thought and practicing *yoga* of the self. (19)

Where restrained by the practice of *yoga*, all thought becomes quiet, and where seeing the self through the self alone, one finds satisfaction within the self. (20)

The infinite joy is grasped by the intellect, while lying beyond the senses; when one knows it, one abides there and never deviates from that reality. (21)

And obtaining which, he counts no other gain as higher; being established in which, he is unmoved even by extreme pain. (22)

Let the severance of contact with pain be known by the name of *yoga*; this *yoga* should be practiced with firm resolve, with mind undaunted. (23)

Having entirely abandoned all desires aroused by willful intent, having controlled the village of the senses on every side by the mind alone, (24)

Let him gradually attain quietude through an intellect set in firmness; having established the mind in the self, he should think of nothing at all. (25)

Whatever makes the fickle and unsteady mind stray, let him withdraw it from those and bring it under the control of the self alone. (26)

For perfect happiness comes to the yogi whose mind has become tranquil, whose passion is calmed, who is without blemish, and who has become one with *Brahman*. (27)

Thus devoting himself to *yoga* constantly, the yogi, freed from blemishes, easily attains contact with *Brahman*, which is infinite joy. (28)

He, whose self is established in *yoga*, who sees sameness in all things, sees himself as abiding in all creatures and all creatures in himself. (29)

He, who sees me everywhere and sees everything in me, is not lost for me and I am not lost for him. (30)

Established in oneness, he who worships me as existing in all creatures; wherever he lives, that yogi lives in me. (31)

One who sees every being as the same, be it in pleasure or pain, through the comparison with himself, he is deemed the highest yogi, O Arjuna. (32)

Arjuna said:

You describe this *yoga* as characterized by sameness, O slayer of demon Madhu; but I do not see its steady endurance due to unsteadiness (of mind). (33)

For the mind is indeed unsteady, O Krishna, impetuous, strong and stubborn; I find it as difficult to restrain as the wind. (34)

The blessed one said:

Without doubt, O mighty-armed (Arjuna), the mind is unsteady and hard to control, but by practice and by non-attachment, O son of Kunti (Arjuna), it can be controlled. (35)

In my view, *yoga* is hard to achieve by one whose self is not controlled, but it is possible to be achieved through proper means by a person of self-mastery who strives for it. (36)

Arjuna said:

A man endowed with faith but no adequate effort, whose mind deviates from *yoga*, not having attained perfection in *yoga*, what path does he tread then, O Krishna? (37)

O mighty-armed, fallen from both, does he not perish like a perforated cloud, unstable, deluded on the path of *Brahman*? (38)

O Krishna, please completely resolve this doubt of mine for there is no one but you who can dispel this doubt. (39)

The blessed one said:

O son of Pritha (Arjuna), there is no destruction for him either in this world or the next, for no one who does good, dear friend, comes to a bad end. (40)

Having attained the worlds made by his virtue, and dwelling there for countless years, the man who has fallen in *yoga* is born in the house of the pure and noble. (41)

Or he is born in a family of yogis endowed with wisdom; though a birth like this is harder to attain in the world. (42)

There he regains the disposition of intellect associated with his former body, and O joy of the Kurus (Arjuna), strives once more for perfection. (43)

For by the force of his former practice itself, he is carried forward even against his wish; even one who (merely) wishes to know the *yoga*, passes beyond the Vedic rites that express *Brahman* in words. (44)

But the yogi who strives with effort, who is purified of all his sins, who attains perfection through many births, thereby reaches the highest goal. (45)

The yogi is superior to men of austerity, he is held to be superior to even the men of knowledge; he is also superior to men of (ritual) action; therefore, be a yogi, O Arjuna! (46)

And of all the yogis, I hold him most disciplined (in *yoga*) who worships me with a faithful heart, with his inner self absorbed in me. (47)

Philosopher's corner: Chapter analysis and questions for consideration

In meditation a yogi is to bring her phenomenal self—the everyday self of names, identities, and diverse roles given in her various engagements and transactions with the external world—in conformity with the real self that transcends this diversity and exists equally in all of us. So sustained practice of meditation enables a practitioner to restrain the senses, control the mind, turn its focus on the transcendent self within, and, thereby, "establish the mind in the self" (6.25). But what does it mean to restrain the mind, to make it such that it becomes "like a lamp which does not flicker [when placed] in a windless place" (6.19)? Krishna elaborates, "all thought becomes quiet"[1] (6.20) and a yogi attains a place where one "should think of nothing at all" (6.25). Is Krishna here asking the yogi to completely disengage and aspire to a mind that is empty? While that might be the prima facie reading, a more consistent and charitable reading would be to take Krishna as advising the yogi to engage with the world with an attitude of equanimity especially since such a yogi is set apart by his "even temperament toward well-wishers, friends, and foes," and toward both good and evil doers (6.9). Again, since the yogi is further marked by his ability to see the "sameness in all things" and "sees himself as abiding in all creatures and all creatures in himself" (6.29) this does not point to a world-renouncing disengagement. Rather, in seeing the unity abiding at the core of every creature the goal is to cultivate a certain attitude of engagement—of non-attachment and equanimity—in relation to everything.

This question about the exact import of Krishna's advice for the yogis also becomes relevant if we take into account the fact that in Western philosophy the defining characteristic of the mental realm is often taken to be its intentionality or aboutness. Unlike the physical realm which is not about anything else (a rock is only ever a rock, a hand is only ever a hand), the mark of the mental appears to be its ability to be about something else. For instance, the mind commonly considers things other than itself, or, in other words, thinks *about* other things: books, food, the Taj Mahal, etc. Now, in asking us to restrain the mind, to make the mind quiet, is the *Gita* asking us to suspend this very intentionality of the mind? In urging us to strive to think of nothing at all, the *Gita* thus presents a unique challenge: how to think about the functioning of a mind that has refocused its directionality. In the light of the preceding discussion we can argue that the project here is not to make the mind empty of thoughts and other states, in the sense of having thoughts without any intentional content, but to make the mind steady in such a way that it does not cling to a specific thought, desire, or feeling. It is also important to note here Arjuna's question as to how to bring about equanimity given the "unsteadiness" (6.33) of the mind. Given the diversity of the intentional content of our mental world Arjuna finds it very challenging to cultivate the attitude of sameness that Krishna recommends. Krishna's response, "by practice and by non-attachment" (6.35), gives support to the reading that the project here is not to achieve a contentless or vacuous mind but to work toward a mind that is marked by non-attachment and even temperament.

Another important philosophically relevant topic from this chapter has to do with the general understanding of the embodied nature of the mind that the *Gita* offers. In outlining the specific methods of the practice of meditation, Krishna not only addresses how the body, neck, and head need to be aligned but also where the gaze should be focused (6.13). He also highlights the importance of surroundings in terms of finding a proper place with the right implements (6.11). Instead of the dualism between mind and body that focuses on their discontinuousness, common-place in Western philosophy of mind, meditation aimed at controlling the mind here nonetheless emphasizes aspects of the body—its posture, gaze, and surrounding. The role of moderation in its multiple dimensions is also emphasized. Thus Krishna advises that the seat of the meditator should be "neither very high nor very low" (11) and the manner of the yogi should be of moderation "in food and recreation," in "efforts in action," and "in sleep and waking" (6.17). This emphasis on moderation provides us with an opportunity to compare the *Gita*'s ethics with the Buddhist idea of middle path viewed as the middle point between the two extremes of self-indulgence and self-mortification and the Aristotelean theme of the golden mean where courage, for example, is viewed as the mean between bravado and cowardice.

This chapter also provides a glimpse into a debate relating rebirth and the karma theory that is internal to some of the Indian schools of philosophy. While rebirth is accepted in all major schools, there remains a disagreement between defenders of the "species continuity" and "cross-species continuity" views when it comes to determining one's next station in the cycle of rebirth. Species continuity is the view that a human being is guaranteed a human form in the next life while cross-species view does not accommodate any such guarantee. Krishna's assurance to Arjuna in verse 6.43 that as a yogi "he is guaranteed a birth that will allow his practice to continue from the point achieved in the previous life" (Phillips 2009, 290) is taken as a support for species continuity. However, it remains an open question whether Krishna guarantees species continuity for every human being (see Phillips 2009, 104–105).

Finally, some contemporary philosophers writing on peace and non-violence focus on the role of meditation and the *yoga* of meditation in the philosophy of non-violence. This chapter thus assumes relevance especially since, having introduced the theme of *samatvam* or equanimity earlier, the *Gita* in this chapter uses it to imply the theme of non-injury and non-harmfulness as the yogi "sees identity in everything" (6.32). It is interesting to note what Joseph Kunkel (2006) shares in his "The Spiritual Side of peacemaking" where he discusses the effects on the students of his course on the Philosophy of Peace by starting every class meeting with a brief meditation exercise. He writes, "the meditation exercises resulted in students learning to examine and interact with the workings of their conscious life" (Kunkel 2006, 32). This in turn allowed them to develop self-control which they then came to realize as an important aspect of being non-violent and peaceful.

Note

1 This theme becomes the central ideal of *Yoga-Sutra*'s understanding of yoga in terms of *citta-vritti-nirodha* or quietening of the modifications of the mind. I thank Stephen Phillips for helping me see this point.

7

The Yoga of Knowledge and Judgment

Summary

This chapter opens with Krishna offering Arjuna a complete knowledge of his nature, of the "material and divine domains" of his nature. In the process he develops the ontologically foundational principle of Prakriti. Until this chapter he has mentioned Prakriti a few times but it is here that he clarifies not only the nature of Prakriti but also the central role that this concept plays in the *Gita*'s overall metaphysics. Krishna's first claim characterizes Prakriti as his ("my") Prakriti. He also identifies the Prakriti as his lower nature thereby differentiating it from his higher nature which he identifies as his "transcendent nature" that is "unchanging and unsurpassed." Prakriti is differentiated into eightfold items, including earth, water, air, fire, mind, intellect, and individuality providing the basic materials—building blocks—of our universe. Prakriti is further taken to be composed of *gunas* through which all the multiplicities of the universe are explained. The knowledge that Krishna elucidates in this chapter captures his nature as the essence of and excellence in every aspect of our phenomenal reality. Krishna assures

Arjuna that this knowledge will set him free from his delusions that are caused by not realizing that our mundane world of myriad things is supported and sustained by the transcendent reality, his higher nature.

The blessed one (Krishna) said:

Listen, O son of Pritha (Arjuna), how, with your mind attached to me, practicing *yoga*, having taken refuge in me, you will know me completely, without doubt! (1)

I will teach you fully this knowledge along with (practical) judgment; having known this, nothing more in this world remains to be known. (2)

Among thousands of men, perhaps one strives for perfection (in spiritual attainment), and, of those who strive and succeed, perhaps one knows me in essence. (3)

My Prakriti has eight-fold differentiations: earth, water, fire, air, space, mind, intellect and ego or individuality. (4)

This is my lower nature but know my different and higher nature too, O mighty-armed (Arjuna)—the life-force and that which sustains the universe. (5)

Know that this is the womb of all beings; I am the origin and also the dissolution of the entire universe. (6)

O Dhananjaya (Arjuna), there is nothing higher than me; all this (universe) is strung on me, like a web of pearls on a string. (7)

O son of Kunti (Arjuna), I am the taste in water, I am the light in the moon and sun; I am the (syllable) OM in all the Vedas, the sound in space and manliness in men. (8)

I am also the pure fragrance in earth, and the radiance in fire; I am the life in all beings and the austerity in ascetics. (9)

Know me to be the eternal seed of all beings, O son of Pritha; I am the intellect of intelligent men and also the splendor of the splendid (heroes). (10)

Of strong men, O bull of the Bharatas (Arjuna), I am the strength (that is) free from longings and attachment; in beings, I am that desire which is not incompatible with *dharma*. (11)

Know that all manifestations of lucidity (*sattva*), passion (*rajas*) and dark inertia (*tamas*) come from me alone; but I am not in them, they are in me. (12)

Deluded by these three states composed of the *gunas*, the entire universe does not recognize me who is beyond them and unchangeable. (13)

For this is my divine *maya* composed of the *gunas* that is hard to overcome; those who take refuge in me alone, pass beyond this *maya*. (14)

The lowest of men, deluded sinners fail to take refuge in me; their knowledge is ruined by *maya*, their nature demonic. (15)

O bull of the Bharatas, four types of virtuous men worship me: the tormented, the knowledge seeker, the wealth seeker, and the wise, O Arjuna. (16)

Of these the wise one excels, being ever disciplined in *yoga* and of singular devotion; for I am exceedingly dear to the wise and he is to me. (17)

All these men are indeed noble but I regard the wise to be my very self; for with his self disciplined in *yoga*, he is established in me alone as his highest way. (18)

At the end of many births, the man of knowledge finds refuge in me realizing that "Vasudeva (Krishna) is all"; that great self is rare to find. (19)

(But others) deprived of knowledge by this or that desire take refuge in other gods, observing various rites, being constrained by their own inclinations. (20)

Whatever form (of deity) a devotee strives faithfully to worship, it is I who make such faith unwavering toward that form. (21)

United with that devotion, he seeks to worship that form (of deity); and from it gains his desires for those are ordained by me alone. (22)

But finite are the results obtained by the men of little intelligence; the worshippers of gods go to the gods while my devotees come to me. (23)

Fools think of me to be the unmanifest that has become manifest; not knowing my transcendent nature, which is unchanging and unsurpassed. (24)

Remaining veiled in the *yoga* of my *maya* I am not revealed to all; this deluded world does not recognize me, the unborn and immutable. (25)

I know all beings of the past, the present, and those who are yet to be; but, O Arjuna, no one knows me. (26)

O Bharata (Arjuna), being deluded by the dualities arising from desire and hatred, all beings are subject to confusion at birth, O scorcher of enemies (Arjuna). (27)

But the men of virtuous deeds, with their sins obliterated, being freed from the delusion of duality, worship me with firm resolve. (28)

Those who strive for freedom from old age and death by taking refuge in me know this *Brahman* entirely and the supreme self and all action. (29)

Those who know me together with (my) material and divine domains and with the supreme sacrifice, becoming disciplined in their minds, continue to know me even at the time of death. (30)

Philosopher's corner: Chapter analysis and questions for consideration

After outlining the basic constituents of his lower nature or Prakriti, Krishna clarifies that under the influence of the incredible diversity of our phenomenal world we come to think that that is all there is. Therefore we fail to see the "unchanging" (7.24), "unborn and immutable" (7.25) source behind this manifold that Krishna identifies as his higher nature (7.13). As an extension of this failure we also fail to realize that Krishna through his higher nature becomes the essential property of everything thereby sustaining the universe (7.5). Therefore, a knowledge of Krishna's complete nature would involve the realization of him being the source of all the myriad things and the changes they go through in the universe *and* the constant resting place of everything thereby providing their ultimate unity. In previous chapters Krishna has used the notion of self in making this point. In making the same case by using his higher and lower natures in this chapter he clarifies that his nature is same as the self or the *Brahman*.

While elaborating on the nature of Prakriti and how it deludes the ordinary, unenlightened mind, Krishna introduces a subtle way of differentiating between desires. Most of our desires, for example, my desire for a clear understanding of the *Gita*, or Arjuna's desire to spare his cousins, operate within our phenomenal reality thereby aiming at a finite and varied outcome (7.23). They are to be overcome since they delude us, according to Krishna, by confining us to the realm of dualities (7.27) and thereby obstructing the realization of the sameness of the transcendent reality of Krishna that is beyond all dualities and changing multiplicities (7.24). This does not imply the rejection of all desires however. When Krishna claims, "I am that desire which is not incompatible with *dharma*" (7.11), he seems to be hinting at those desires that are not marked by everyday dualities and finitudes. Thus the desire represented in the yogi's "strive for freedom from old age and death by taking refuge in ... [Krishna]" is of a kind that is valuable since it is necessary for the attainment of the highest good, namely, conscious unity with Krishna and *Brahman* (7.29). Further, since the pursuit of this kind of desire requires sustained cultivation through *yoga*, Krishna is also making the case that at least some desires require disciplined cultivation and are not automatically given. Finally, while Krishna does not provide a taxonomy of desires here, by offering a way to differentiate between acceptable and deluded desires he does invite us to problematize the topics of equanimity and non-attachment and the role of desires in their development.

8

The Yoga of the Imperishable *Brahman*

Summary

This chapter opens with Arjuna's request for clarification in relation to a number of metaphysical concepts that Krishna has introduced so far, namely, that of *Brahman*, self, action, and his material and divine domains. In response Krishna reiterates and further extends the idea that he is the self, the "inherent nature," existing in every being, that he is the same as *Brahman* and that he is the "creative power that causes the origin of the states of beings" in action. Krishna elaborates further on his two natures: his lower nature or Prakriti that is the location and cause of all change and multiplicities and therefore "perishable," and his higher or transcendent nature that remains unchanged and immutable. He identifies this transcendent principle with *Brahman* as well as the Purusha or spirit. This chapter refers to a number of Hindu themes on the topics of cosmic cycles, rebirth, and how a time of death, namely, whether one dies during the months following the winter solstice or during the months following the summer solstice, determines the next station, and finally how one attains liberation. Drawing from these Krishna outlines the state of mind and consciousness of a yogi who is able to remain unwavering in focus on Krishna through lifelong cultivation of *yoga* at the time of death, thereby reaching the highest goal of attaining Krishna and freedom from the cycle of rebirth—"the abode of suffering and impermanence."

Arjuna said:

O best of the Purushas, what is *Brahman*? What is the self? What is action? What is called the material domain? What is said to be the divine domain? (1)

Who is the supreme sacrifice, O slayer of demon Madhu? How does he live here in this body? And how are you to be known by men of self-control at the time of death? (2)

The blessed one (Krishna) said:

Indestructible and supreme is *Brahman*; the self (in the individual) is called its inherent nature; its creative power that causes the origin of the states of beings is called action. (3)

The basis of all perishable things is material and the Purusha (sprit) is the divine; I am the supreme sacrifice here in the body, O best of the embodied ones (Arjuna)! (4)

And anyone, who goes forth remembering me alone at the time of death, enters my being after leaving the body; of this there is no doubt. (5)

O son of Kunti (Arjuna), whatever state of being a man remembers while leaving his body at the time of death, to that state alone he enters due to his ever persistence in it. (6)

Therefore, remember me at all times and fight; with your mind and understanding fixed on me, you will come to me without a doubt. (7)

O son of Pritha (Arjuna), the man whose reason is disciplined in the *yoga* of practice and never strays to another object, will reach the supreme divine Purusha (spirit) while meditating thereon. (8)

He who remembers the Purusha (spirit) as the primordial poet, smaller than the finest atom, supporter of all and the great ruler, as one whose form is inconceivable, who is the color of the sun, beyond darkness, (9)

At the time of death, this man, with his mind unshakable, united by devotion and the strength of the *yoga*, focusing his vital breath between the eyebrows, attains that supreme divine Purusha (spirit). (10)

I will explain to you in summary that place which the Vedic scholars describe as immutable, which the ascetics enter being freed from attachment, and seeking which they lead a celibate life. (11)

Having controlled all of the body's gates, and cloistering the mind in the heart, placing one's own breath in the head, establishing oneself in the steady practice of *yoga*, (12)

Uttering OM, the one eternal syllable of *Brahman*, remembering me as he departs and leaves his body, he reaches the highest goal. (13)

O son of Pritha, I am easily attained by that yogi who focuses on nothing else (but me), remembers me constantly, and who is ever-disciplined in *yoga*. (14)

Having obtained me, men of great spirit do not undergo rebirth—the abode of suffering and impermanence; they attain highest perfection. (15)

O Arjuna, worlds even up to Brahma's cosmic realm are for those who will return again; but on reaching me there is no rebirth, O son of Kunti. (16)

Those who know that a day of Brahma stretches over a thousand cycles, and his night lasts for another thousand cycles, are the people who know what day and night are. (17)

At the break of Brahma's day all manifest entities come forth from the unmanifest; at the dusk of Brahma's night, they dissolve back into the same which is called the unmanifest. (18)

O son of Pritha, after being born again and again the very same multitude of beings dissolves willy-nilly at nightfall to emerge again at the approach of day. (19)

Even higher than this unmanifest nature is another unmanifest eternal existence, that does not perish when all beings perish. (20)

This unmanifest which is called the imperishable, is also what they call the highest goal; those who attain it—my supreme abode—undergo no more rebirth. (21)

O son of Pritha, by singular devotion that supreme Purusha (spirit) can be reached, in whom (all) beings abide and by whom the whole universe is pervaded. (22)

O bull of the Bharatas (Arjuna), I will tell you precisely the time departing in which the dying yogis never return and also the time departing in which they do return. (23)

Dying in fire, light, day, the bright (fortnight of the moon) and the sun's six-month northward course, men who know *Brahman* go onto *Brahman*. (24)

(Dying) in smoke, night, the dark (fortnight of the moon), and the sun's six-month southward course, a yogi obtains the lunar light and then returns (to be reborn). (25)

For these two courses—the bright and the dark—are deemed eternal in the universe; by one, one goes never to return, by the other, one returns (to be born) again. (26)

Knowing these two paths, O son of Pritha, no yogi is deluded; therefore, O Arjuna, at all times discipline yourself firmly in *yoga*. (27)

Having known all this the yogi transcends the fruit of virtue declared in the Vedas, in sacrifices, in austerities and in acts of charity, and ascends to the highest primeval place. (28)

Philosopher's corner: Chapter analysis and questions for consideration

Krishna presents Purusha and Prakriti as his two aspects or two natures. This portrayal thus seems to attempt to transcend the dualism prominent in some schools of Hindu philosophy, Samkhya for example, that consider Prakriti and Purusha as two distinct ontological entities. It remains unclear, however, how these two natures might interact or what could be the mechanism of such an interaction. It is also an interesting question to consider what Krishna's exact relation is to these two natures. Does he stand over and above them or is he constituted by these two natures? If the latter, does that make his own nature divisible? Further, how important it is to answer these metaphysical questions for a full delineation of the liberating knowledge that Krishna recommended in Chapter 7.

Krishna seems to explain the mechanics underlying the Hindu concepts of rebirth and karma here. The basic idea, as Krishna introduced in Chapter 2, is that every individual goes through numerous rebirths after the death of the present body unless he has already realized his sameness with Krishna. One's next birth is determined by the karmic residues of one's actions in present and past lives. In this chapter Krishna further proposes, "whatever state of being a man remembers while leaving his body at the time of death, to that state alone he enters due to his ever persistence in it" (8.6). His suggestion here that one's mental states at the time of death determine the form of rebirth in the next life can be taken as the *Gita*'s effort to operationalize the relationship between karmic residue and rebirth. Like the statement, "you are what you eat," the *Gita* here seems to be suggesting, "You will be what you think and focus on especially at the time of death." So if a yogi's mind is focused on Krishna *alone* at the time of his death—however hard it might be to attain that kind of purity of thought—then he attains Krishna after death (8.13). The reason a yogi's mind might be so focused is because one's mental world is shaped by one's disposition and cultivation of mental attitudes up to that point. That is to say, the makeup of one's karmic residue count at one moment in turn determines one's mental content and attitude in the next moment so that the mental state at the time of death is shaped by one's previous mental discipline and cultivation of attitudes like non-attachment. So since a yogi "focuses on nothing else [but Krishna], remembers [him] constantly" (8.14), his mental reality is such that he will be focused on Krishna at the time of death. Such a yogi will thus attain *Brahman*, Krishna's "supreme abode" (8.21), and will be freed from the cycle of rebirths (8.15). Drawing from other Hindu scriptural sources, the *Gita* tries to enumerate certain signs, for example, "sun's six-month northward course" (8.24), to indicate whether a yogi while dying during that period will attain freedom from rebirth.

Finally, in this chapter Krishna also reiterates that it is not only the case that individuals go through the cycles of rebirths but that the entire creation goes through cycles; from Krishna's unmanifest nature all manifest entities issue forth at the beginning of evolution only to "dissolve back into the same" unmanifest (8.18) and this process continues without end (see also 9.10 in this regard).

9

The Yoga of Sovereign Science and Sovereign Secret

Summary

In this chapter Krishna comes closest to presenting himself as the creator God in declaring that using his "divine *yoga*," which he identified with *maya* in Chapter 7, and his lower nature or Prakriti, he sends forth all beings "at the beginning of the (next) world-cycle" after everything is returned to his Prakriti at the end of a world-cycle thereby creating everything in alternative cycles. This, of course, is in keeping with his transcendent nature which serves as the "originator and sustainer of all beings." In Chapter 8 Krishna also identified himself as the essence and excellence in a variety of things. In the present chapter he elaborates on this theme by expanding the list by including the medicinal herb, the threefold Vedas, and the immortality as well as death among numerous others. He also seems to present himself as the sole and single reality behind the diversity of gods and goddesses of the Hindu pantheon. The last part of this chapter turns to developing the theme of devotion to

Krishna and hints at the significance it is going to assume in Krishna's overall ethical counsel in the *Gita*. Nowhere is this more evident than in Krishna's assurance that even an "exceedingly wicked person" becomes virtuous when he worships Krishna with "undeviating devotion." Krishna also highlights the inclusive power of devotion as a means to spiritual freedom since it, unlike some of the other means like the *yoga* of knowledge or renunciation, is easily available to many on the periphery and the margins of the Hindu society.

The blessed one (Krishna) said:

But now I will teach the deepest mystery to you since you are uncomplaining; realizing it with knowledge and discernment, you will be freed from evil. (1)

This is the king of sciences, the royal mystery, the supreme purifier; realizable through direct experience, the essence of *dharma*, joy to perform and unchanging. (2)

Men without faith in this *dharma* fail to attain me, O Scorcher of foes (Arjuna); they return to the endless cycle of death and rebirth. (3)

This entire universe is pervaded by me in my unmanifest form; all beings abide in me but I do not abide in them. (4)

And (yet) beings do not abide in me; behold my divine *yoga*; though my self is the originator and sustainer of all beings, it does not abide in them. (5)

Understand it thus: just as freely-moving mighty air constantly abides in space, so all beings abide in me. (6)

At the end of a world-cycle (kalpa), O son of Kunti (Arjuna), all beings enter into my Prakriti; I send them forth again at the beginning of the (next) world-cycle. (7)

Animating my Prakriti, again and again I send forth this whole host of beings, (rendered) powerless by the force of (my) Prakriti. (8)

O Dhananjaya (Arjuna), nor do these actions bind me (since) I remain unattached in all my actions, as if standing apart (and therefore aloof) from them. (9)

O son of Kunti, with me as the overseer the Prakriti gives birth to all the animate and inanimate beings; and because of this the universe revolves in alternating cycles. (10)

Fools despise me in the human form I have assumed, not knowing my higher nature as the great lord of beings. (11)

Lacking in insight, their desires, actions and knowledge all vain, they take refuge in the seductive, devilish and demonic nature. (12)

But O son of Pritha (Arjuna), great souls, abiding in the divine nature, worship me with unwavering mind, knowing (me as) the imperishable source of beings. (13)

Always glorifying me and striving with firm resolve, (my devotees) bow down to me with devotion and worship me being ever disciplined (in *yoga*). (14)

Yet others, offering the sacrifice of knowledge, worship me in various ways—as the one, as the distinct (in my manifold forms), and as one facing in all directions. (15)

I am the rite, I am the sacrifice, I am the offering to the dead, I am the medicinal herb, I am the sacred chant, I alone am the clarified butter, I am the fire, (and) I am the oblation. (16)

I am the father of this universe, the mother, the ordainer, the grandfather; the object of knowledge, the purifier, the holy syllable OM, and the threefold Vedas: Rig, Sama and Yajur. (17)

I am the goal, the sustainer, the lord, the witness; the abode, refuge, (and) friend; (I am) the origin, dissolution, foundation, treasure (and) the indestructible seed. (18)

I give heat, I withhold and send down the rains; I am immortality as well as death, I am both being and non-being, O Arjuna! (19)

Men, knowers of the three Vedas, drinkers of the Soma, being purified of their sins, worship me with sacrifices, seeking to win the way to heaven; attaining the holy world of Indra (king of the gods), they taste the divine delights of the gods in the celestial sphere. (20)

After enjoying the vast world of the heaven, they (re-)enter the mortal world when their merits have been exhausted; thus following the *dharmas* enjoined in the three Vedas, desiring desires, they attain what is transient. (21)

Men, who worship me (only) without thinking of any other, who are ever united in me with constant *yoga*; their prosperity and welfare are provided by me. (22)

O son of Kunti (Arjuna), even devotees of other gods, who endowed with faith sacrifice to them, even they sacrifice to me alone, though not in the proper way. (23)

For I am the recipient and also the lord of all sacrifices; but they do not recognize me in reality and so they fall (i.e., are reborn). (24)

Devotees of the gods go to the gods, ancestor-worshippers go to the ancestors; those who worship spirits go to them and my worshippers come to me. (25)

Whoever offers me a leaf or a flower or a fruit or water with devotion, I accept that offering of devotion of the pure at heart. (26)

O son of Kunti, whatever you do—whether in eating, whether in observing spiritual rites, whether in giving or in performing austerities—dedicate that as an offering to me. (27)

Thus you will be freed from the bonds of action, from its good and bad fruits; with your self disciplined in the *yoga* of renunciation, liberated, you will come to me. (28)

I am the same to all beings, there is no one either hateful or dear to me; but those who worship me with devotion, they are in me and I am in them as well. (29)

Even an exceedingly wicked person, if he worships me with undeviating devotion, must indeed be regarded as virtuous for he has the right resolve. (30)

He will soon become a person of *dharma* and attain eternal peace; O son of Kunti, know this to be a fact: my devotee never perishes. (31)

For by taking refuge in me, O son of Pritha, even those who may be born of sinful wombs, women, members of the vaisya caste (business caste) or even a member of the sudra caste (servant caste), can reach the highest goal as well. (32)

How much (easier for) holy brahmins (members of the priest caste) and devoted royal sages; having come into this transient, unhappy world, devote yourself to me! (33)

Focus your mind on me, be my devotee, sacrifice to me, bow to me; having thus disciplined yourself, taking me as the highest goal, you will come only to me. (34)

Philosopher's corner: Chapter analysis
and questions for consideration

In her Introduction to this chapter Diana Morrison writes, "It [Chapter 9] contains *no philosophy* and only a little theology. The one message is: anyone who has real love, love for the Lord of Love who is in all creatures, will in the end attain the goal" (in Easwaran (2007) 172, italicized emphasis added). Morrison's estimation would be correct only if we apply a rather narrow understanding of philosophy that especially excludes comparative philosophy and aspects of Hindu philosophy. Given Krishna's identifying himself as the creator God of the universe, he could be compared with the Judeo-Christian God or the God of theism, one of whose defining marks is being the creator of the universe. In that capacity God also transcends his creation and provides support for his creation. But there will be a few challenges to any straightforward comparison between Krishna and the God of theism. First of all, Krishna is a human being, a dear friend of Arjuna and therefore quite unlike the God of theism. Secondly, the long list of sacred inanimate and animate things and roles that Krishna identifies himself with (9.16 through 9.19) also poses challenge to any prima facie comparison. Finally, it is interesting to note how the topic of heaven enters into the discussion here. While heaven is commonly understood as the final destination where people experience perfect harmony with God and with each other within the context of Christianity or Islam, heaven is treated by Krishna as part of the rebirth cycle, thereby ultimately as a part of the transient world. As Krishna clarifies, through performance of Vedic rituals people "win the way to heaven" (9.20) only to "(re-)enter the mortal world when their [karmic] merits have been exhausted" (9.21). So it is not heaven but the highest goal of becoming one with Krishna that serves as the final resting place in this system of the *Gita.* This final destination also renders Krishna, even in his higher nature, not completely transcendent. Interestingly, since the creator aspect of Krishna is being emphasized in this chapter—as evident in his proclamation "all beings abide in me but I do not abide in them" (9.4)—the idea that Krishna exists in all beings—an idea emphasized in other chapters, see, for example, 10.20—is unacknowledged here.

Krishna also focuses on articulating how the universe relates to his divine powers and how a clear knowledge of this "deepest mystery" (9.1) features in the human-divine relationship. This chapter thus introduces one of *Gita's* most prominent contributions to Hindu philosophy in terms of a clear articulation of a personal God and a delineation of a human-divine relationship. Krishna praises those who worship him "in his divine nature" with a single-minded and unwavering dedication knowing him as the "imperishable source of all creatures" (9.13). In so doing he introduces and highlights one of the central tenets of the *Gita*, namely, devotion as the primary means of attaining union with Krishna. A few distinguishing marks of devotion are outlined. First, devotion involves an offering and is determined by the purity of heart and not by the value of the object being offered. Thus, even "a leaf or a flower or a fruit or water" when offered with a pure heart and unwavering dedication becomes accepted as an "offering of devotion" (9.26). Next, the most prominent feature of a person of devotion is that she takes refuge in Krishna (9.32). As Krishna elaborates, such a person performs *all* her actions as offerings dedicated to Krishna and consequently all her actions are "freed from the bonds of action" (9.28). Thus the refuge in Krishna produces the same results as performing action without attachment even though one might not have perfected the *yoga* of action or knowledge. This seems to enable even people of lowly origins according to traditional Hindu understanding, women or Sudras for example, who are otherwise undeserving of the highest goal of becoming one with Krishna to reach the highest goal (9.32). The prominence of devotion as a path to attaining Krishna is unmistakable. In fact, even the knowledge that is identified as the "deepest mystery" is realized only through "direct experience" by one who is devoted to Krishna. Indeed those who offer their worship and sacrifices to other gods also end up worshipping Krishna alone—without realizing it—as he is the "lord of all sacrifices" (9.24) and the "great lord of beings" (9.11). Thus the different Vedas and the Hindu polytheistic system get subsumed under Krishna's unifying nature here. In so doing this chapter clearly embodies a philosophical and methodological synthesis between various strands of Hindu religious and philosophical systems.

10

The Yoga of Divine Manifestations

Summary

Until this chapter Arjuna's questions to Krishna centered on clarification, further explanation, and even some puzzlement (see, for example, 4.4). However, Chapter 10 marks a clear shift. For the first time Arjuna seems convinced not only of Krishna's divine status but also of his being the "supreme *Brahman*." Similarly unlike Chapter 9 that highlighted Krishna's higher or transcendent nature, this chapter focuses on his immanent nature through which he pervades everything. Building on the theme introduced in Chapters 8 and 9 of Krishna being the essence and excellence in everything, he lists an amazingly wide range—from his being "the self dwelling in the heart of all beings," and the best horse to Yama, the god of death—as an illustration of his divine manifestations. The chapter concludes with Krishna's unequivocal declaration that even a hint of power, grace, and vigor in anything comes only from a mere fraction of his brilliance.

The blessed one (Krishna) said:

O mighty-armed (Arjuna), hear again my supreme word; desiring your well-being I will declare this to you for your delight. (1)

Neither the multitude of gods nor the great sages know my origin, for I am the source of all the gods and the great sages in every way. (2)

A man, who knows me as the unborn and beginningless, and the great lord of the world, is undeluded among mortals and is freed from all evils. (3)

Understanding, knowledge, non-delusion, forgiveness, truth, control (of the senses), tranquility, happiness, sorrow, arising, passing away, fear, and fearlessness as well, (4)

Nonviolence, equanimity, contentedness, austerity, charity, fame and infamy—(these) diverse states of beings arise from me alone. (5)

The seven ancient great sages and the four Manus (ancestors of humanity) are modifications of my nature, born of my mind; from these (progenitors) come all creatures of this world. (6)

The man, who truly knows this supernal manifestation and this *yoga* of mine, is united with me by unwavering *yoga*; in this there is no doubt. (7)

I am the source of all, everything proceeds from me; realizing thus the wise worship me, filled with my being. (8)

Their thoughts fully on me, their beings surrendered to me, enlightening one another and constantly proclaiming me, they (my devotees) are joyous and delighted. (9)

To men thus ever united with me and worshipping me with love, I give the *yoga* of understanding, by which they come to me. (10)

Out of compassion for them (while) remaining in my own nature, I dispel the darkness born of ignorance with the luminous lamp of knowledge. (11)

Arjuna said:

You are the supreme *Brahman*, the supreme abode, the sublime purity, Purusha, the eternal, divine (and) primordial god, the unborn lord, (12)

Thus all the great sages, the divine seer Narada, and Asita, Devala and Vyasa (epic poet) spoke of you; and now you yourself declare it to me. (13)

O handsome-haired one, I accept all this you tell me to be true; for, O lord, neither the gods nor the demons know your manifestation. (14)

O Supreme Person, O Sustainer of the beings, O Lord of all beings, O God of gods, O Ruler of the universe, you know yourself through yourself alone. (15)

Please tell me without reserve, I implore you, for divine are the manifestations of your self, by which manifestations you remain pervading these worlds. (16)

O great yogi, how may I know you by constant meditation? And in what diverse states of being are you to be imagined by me, O lord? (17)

O Janardana, explain again in full extent the *yoga* and supernal manifestation of your self; for never can I have enough of the immortal nectar of your speech. (18)

The blessed one said:

O best of the Kurus (Arjuna), come then, I will tell you the divine supernal manifestations of my self, but only the important ones for there is no end to my extent. (19)

O thick-haired one (Arjuna)! I am the self dwelling in the heart of all beings; I am also their beginning, their middle, and their end. (20)

Of the Adityas (sun gods) I am Vishnu, of the luminous bodies I am the radiant sun; of the Marutas (wind gods) I am Marichi (lightning), of stars I am the moon. (21)

Of the Vedas I am the Sama Veda (song), of the gods I am Vasava (Indra); of the senses I am the mind, and I am the consciousness of beings. (22)

Of the Rudras (howling storm gods) I am Shankara (Shiva), of Yakshas (demigods) and Rakshasas (goblins) I am Kubera (the lord of wealth); of the Vasus (eight bright gods) I am Pavaka (fire), and of mountain peaks I am Meru. (23)

And, O son of Pritha (Arjuna), of the household priests know me as the chief Brihaspati (teacher of all gods), of war commanders, I am Skanda (the god of war), of bodies of waters I am the ocean. (24)

Of the great sages, I am Bhrigu (the priest of the great sages), of utterances I am the single syllable (OM), among sacrifices, I am the silent prayer; among stationary objects, I am the Himalaya. (25)

Of all trees, I am the ashvattha (the peepal tree), of divine sages, I am Narada (the chief); of heavenly musicians I am Chitraratha (leader), of perfected beings I am sage Kapila. (26)

Of horses, know me as the immortal Uchchaihshravas (Indra's steed), born from nectar; of lordly elephants, the Airavata (the divine king Indra's mount), and of men, the monarch. (27)

Of weapons I am the thunderbolt, of cows I am the Kamadhenu (the magical wish-granting cow); I am Kandarpa (the god of love)—the cause of childbirths, and of serpents I am Vasuki (the king of the snakes). (28)

Of mythical serpents I am the Ananta (endless one), of water creatures I am Varuna (god of the ocean); of dead ancestors I am Aryama (chief); of restraints I am Yama (god of death). (29)

Of demons I am Prahlada (the pious son), of reckoners I am time; of wild animals I am the king of beasts (the lion), and of birds I am Garuda (Vishnu's birdlike mount). (30)

Of purifiers, I am the wind, of wielders of weapons, I am Rama; of sea creatures I am Makara (sea-monster crocodile), of streams I am Jahnavi (the Ganges). (31)

Of creations, O Arjuna, I am the beginning, the middle and also the end; of (all branches of) knowledge I am the wisdom of the self, of those who speak I am the speech. (32)

Of letters I am the letter A and of compounds I am the Dvanda (connective element in forming a word); I myself am indestructible time, I am the creator facing in every direction. (33)

I am death—the all-destroying; I am birth, the origin of all that will be; of feminine powers I am fame, success, speech, memory, intelligence, fortitude, and forgiveness. (34)

Similarly of chants I am Brihat-Saman (great ritual chant), of poetic meters I am Gayatri (ancient meter of twenty-four syllables); of months I am Margasirsha (an auspicious winter month), of seasons I am Kusumakara (flower bearer, spring). (35)

I am the gambling of the cheaters, I am the brilliance of the brilliant; I am victory, I am resolve, I am the courage of the courageous. (36)

Of the mighty kinsmen I am Vasudeva (Krishna), of the Pandava princes I am Dhananjaya (Arjuna); of the sages I am Vyasa (epic poet, author of *Mahabharata*), of the poets I am the savant Ushanas. (37)

I am the scepter of rulers, I am the statesmanship of those that wish to win; of secrets I am also the silence and I am the knowledge of those who know. (38)

Moreover, whatever is the seed of all beings, O Arjuna, I am that; no being, whether animate or inanimate, could exist without me. (39)

There is no limit to my divine supernal manifestations, O fiery hero (Arjuna)! But I have declared only a sampling of the extent of my supernal manifestation. (40)

Whatever being reflects power or grace or vigor, know that to have originated in every case from a (mere) fraction of my brilliance. (41)

But of what use to you, O Arjuna, is this detailed knowledge? I stand sustaining this entire universe with only a single fragment (of my being). (42)

Philosopher's corner: Chapter analysis and questions for consideration

The focus of this chapter is to identify Krishna not only as the source of everything in the universe but also as the element of excellence and the source of power, thereby rendering him as the best, in setting the standard, in every context. He is identified not only with the best in everything that we typically think of as good like the gods and mighty sages, but also as the best among the demons (10.30). Moreover, he is not only identified as the best among the gods, demons, and sages, he is also identified as the best among inanimate objects like the wind (10.31) or the winter month or the spring (10.35). He thus identifies himself as the Himalaya (10.25), the ashvattha or the sacred fig tree (10.26) and as the "gambling of the cheaters" (10.36). He is also not always male as verse 34 clearly characterizes him as "fame, success, speech, memory, intelligence, fortitude and forgiveness" among the "feminine powers." He is also identified as the first letter and other primary elements of language. Given this vast and diverse array of identities, it seems appropriate to investigate the philosophical implication of this multiplicity. Further, is this multiplicity consistent with the other overarching claim of the *Gita* that Krishna is the element of truth in all of us? Other chapters have argued that knowing Krishna allows us to see *everything* with an equal eye, so it is worth exploring what philosophical gain the focus on the multiplicity of this chapter affords. Who might possibly be Krishna's audience in this chapter? Some of the philosophically interesting questions in this regard include, what is the best way to interpret Krishna's "divine supernal manifestations" (10.40) here? In characterizing himself as the element of excellence, is Krishna giving us a pantheistic understanding of himself, while at the same time remaining transcendent as the final two verses clearly attest?

Krishna lists, among other things, nonviolence, equanimity, charity, fame, and infamy as "diverse states of beings" and states that they all arise from him alone (10.5). A number of questions can be asked in this regard. Are these diverse items all "states of beings" in the same sense of the term? Can fame and infamy be states of beings in the same way that non-violence or equanimity or even charity? Especially since equanimity or tranquility, another item on Krishna's list, seems to depend solely on internal cultivation unlike fame or infamy, it is worthwhile to ask how they all belong to the same list. Finally, the exact mechanism through which they all arise from Krishna alone is also an interesting topic to pursue.

11

The Yoga of the Vision of the Cosmic Form

Summary

This chapter shifts its focus from description to demonstration as it opens with Arjuna's desire to *behold* Krishna's infinite form in all its majesty. In the process of fulfilling Arjuna's desire Krishna reveals that this is going to be no simple show and tell given Arjuna's needing a divine eye. With that he is able to *see* Krishna's wondrous "highest sovereign form" of countless arms, bellies, mouths, eyes, feet, and thighs, and terrible fangs "devouring all the world" with his flaming mouths. Arjuna sees "the entire universe together with animate and inanimate things" in this infinite form of Krishna that "fills the space between heaven and earth." All the gods, demons, demigods, and every being lying in between including the heroes on Arjuna's own and his opponent's sides rush into the blazing mouths of Krishna as "moths rush in hurtling haste into a blazing flame." The extraordinary magnitude of this sight is captured in Arjuna's earnest supplication to Krishna to reappear in his gentle human form as he finds his cosmic form distressing to behold for long. Arjuna's numerous venerations of Krishna's glorious and yet terrifying form establish Krishna as the undisputed source of everything, the "Being with

unparalleled power." Krishna also assures Arjuna that the
warriors assembled at the battle field "are already killed"
by Krishna and that Arjuna need only be "an instrument" of
Krishna.Thus this chapter can be read as providing evidence for
claims Krishna made in the previous chapters regarding being
the originator, sustainer, and destroyer of the universe. Finally,
Krishna clarifies that this form is revealed as a pure gift *only* to
a devotee, a person of "unwavering devotion."

Arjuna said:

Out of compassion for me you have revealed the deepest mystery
called the supreme self; by your words my delusion is dispelled.
(1)

For I heard from you in detail the origin and dissolution of beings,
O lotus-petal-eyed one, and also about the self in its inexhaustible
greatness. (2)

This is just as you declared yourself, O supreme lord! O supreme
among men, I desire to behold your form in all its majesty. (3)

If you think it can be beheld by me, O lord, then, O lord of *yoga*, reveal
to me your immutable self. (4)

The blessed one (Krishna) said:

O son of Pritha (Arjuna) behold my forms by the hundreds and by
thousands—manifold, divine, of diverse colors and shapes. (5)

Behold the Adityas (sun gods), the Vasus (gods of light), the Rudras
(howling storm gods), the twin Ashvins (gods of dawn), and also the
Marutas (gods of wind); behold, O Bharata (Arjuna), many wonders
that no one has seen before. (6)

O thick-haired one (Arjuna), behold here today the entire universe
together with animate and inanimate things, and whatever else you
desire to see as they stand as one in my body. (7)

But you cannot see me with your own (mortal) eyes; I will give you a
divine eye. (With that eye) Behold my divine *yoga*. (8)

Sanjaya said:

O king (Dhritarashtra), having spoken thus, Hari, the great lord of *yoga*, then revealed to the son of Pritha his highest sovereign form. (9)

Of countless mouths and eyes, of many wondrous visions, of many divine ornaments, with many divine weapons raised; (10)

Wearing celestial garlands and garments, anointed with celestial perfume, comprised of every wonder; radiant, infinite with faces in all directions. (11)

If a thousand suns were to shine forth in the sky all at once, the resulting splendor may be like the brilliance of that great spirit. (12)

There the son of Pandu (Arjuna) saw the entire universe with its multiple divisions as united (as one) within the body of the god of the gods. (13)

Then filled with wonder, his hair standing up on end, Dhananjaya (Arjuna), bowed his head to the god and spoke with his palms together (in a reverential gesture). (14)

Arjuna said:

O God, I see in your body all the gods and hosts of many kinds of beings: Brahma—the cosmic creator seated on his lotus seat, along with all the seers and celestial serpents. (15)

With countless arms, bellies, mouths and eyes, I behold your infinite form everywhere; I see no end, nor middle nor even beginning to your form, O Lord of the Universe, O Universal Form! (16)

With your crown, mace, and discus, a mass of radiance, blazing on all sides; I behold you, though hard to behold, in the burning light of fire and sun that surrounds your immeasurable (form)! (17)

You are imperishable, supreme object of knowledge, you are the supreme shelter of the universe, you are the immutable protector of eternal *dharma*; you are the primeval Purusha: this is my view. (18)

Without beginning, or middle or end, of boundless strength, of endless arms, the moon and the sun as your eyes, I behold you whose mouth is burning fire scorching this universe with your brilliance. (19)

For the space between heaven and earth and all the directions are pervaded by you alone; seeing this wondrous, terrible form of yours, O Great Spirit, the three worlds tremble! (20)

For these hosts of gods enter you, some in their terror extol you with folded hands (gesture of homage); hosts of great sages and perfected ones hail you with chants of "peace" and praise you with splendorous hymns. (21)

The Rudras (howling storm gods), Adityas (sun gods), Vasus (gods of light) and Sadhyas (gods of ritual), the Viswas (All-gods), Ashvins (the twin gods of dawn), Marutas (wind gods), ushmapas (steam inhaling ancestors), gandharvas (hosts of celestial musicians), yakshas (demigods), demons, and perfected ones gaze at you and are all awestruck. (22)

O Mighty-armed, beholding your great form of the myriad mouths and eyes, of many arms, thighs, and feet, of many bellies and terrible fangs, the worlds tremble and so do I. (23)

When I see you touch the sky being ablaze with many colors, with wide open mouths and huge blazing eyes, my inner self trembles and I find no resolve or tranquility, O Vishnu! (24)

And seeing the terrible fangs protruding from your mouths like the (devouring) fires of time, I know no direction (i.e., no orientation) nor do I find refuge; be gracious, O Lord of Gods, Abode of the Universe! (25)

And (into) you (enter) all these sons of Dhritarashtra, accompanied by hosts of kings, Bhishma, Drona, and the son of the charioteer (Karna) together with our chief warriors as well; (26)

Rushing into your (gaping) mouths, horrifying with terrible fangs, some, caught in the gaps between the teeth, are seen with their heads crushed. (27)

As the many water torrents of the rivers rush headlong into the single sea, so do these heroes of this world of mortals enter into your blazing mouths. (28)

As moths rush in hurtling haste into a blazing flame for destruction, worlds too enter with great speed into your mouths for destruction. (29)

Devouring all the worlds with your flaming mouths, you lick them all around; O Vishnu, filling the entire universe with your brilliance, your violent rays scorch! (30)

Tell me who you are in this terrifying form! O Best of Gods, homage to you, be merciful! I want to know you in your original form because I don't comprehend your ways. (31)

The blessed one said:
I am time (i.e., death), the mighty cause of world destruction, set out to annihilate the worlds here; even without you (i.e., if you don't fight), all these warriors arrayed in opposing ranks will not survive. (32)

Therefore, you arise (and) win glory! Conquering your enemies, you enjoy prosperous kingdoms! They have already been killed by me long ago, O ambidextrous archer (Arjuna), be only my instrument! (33)

Drona and Bhishma and Jayadratha and also Karna, and all the other war heroes as well; you kill them (as) they are already killed by me; do not waver! Fight! You will conquer your enemies in battle. (34)

Sanjaya said:
Hearing these words of the handsome-haired one (Krishna), the crowned one (Arjuna), with his palms joined in reverent homage, trembling, made humble obeisance and addressed Krishna again in a quavering voice, bowing down, being overwhelmed with fear. (35)

Arjuna said:
O Hrishikesha, rightly it is that the universe rejoices and is exceedingly delighted by your glory; terrified demons scatter in all directions and all the hosts of perfected ones bow down in homage. (36)

And why should they not pay homage to you, O Great Spirit? You are greater even than Brahma (who issued from you), you are the first cause; O Infinite Lord of Gods, O Shelter of the Universe, you are imperishable, being, nonbeing and that what is beyond both. (37)

You are the Primal God, the ancient Purusha, you are the ultimate refuge of this universe; you are the knower and what is to be known, and the supreme abode; the universe is pervaded by you, O Being of Boundless Form! (38)

You are Vayu (god of wind), Yama (god of death), Agni (god of fire), Varuna (god of water), you are the moon; you are Prajapati (lord of creatures) and the great grandfather. Homage, homage be to you a thousand times! Homage to you again and yet again, homage! (39)

Homage to you from front and from behind, homage to you from all sides, O All! O Being of Infinite Power and Immeasurable Strength, you accomplish all, therefore you are all. (40)

Whatever I said audaciously, thinking of you as a friend, addressing you as, "Hey, Krishna! Hey, Yadava, hey, friend!," unaware of this majesty of yours, either from carelessness or even through love, (41)

And if I have disrespected you for the sake of a joke while at play, rest, sitting, or at mealtimes, O Unshaken One, either alone or in the presence of others, for that I beg your forgiveness, O Unfathomable One! (42)

You are the father of this world of animate and inanimate things; you are its most venerable teacher and most worthy of worship; there exists no equal to you; how could there be another surpassing you even in the three worlds, O Being of Unparalleled Power? (43)

Therefore, bowing to you (and) prostrating my body at your feet, I beg you to be gracious, O Praiseworthy Lord! As a father to his son, as a friend to his friend, as a lover to his beloved, O God, please be patient with me. (44)

Having seen what has never been seen before I am delighted and yet my mind is distressed with fear. O Lord of Gods, show me that form only (that I know), O Shelter of the Universe, have mercy! (45)

I long to see you as before, wearing the crown, carrying the mace, and with the discus in your hand; appear (again) in that same four-armed form, O Thousand-armed One, of universal form! (46)

The blessed one said:

O Arjuna, by my grace this highest form has been revealed for you through my power of *yoga*; radiant, all-embracing, infinite, primeval (this form) of mine which no one but you has ever seen before. (47)

O great hero of the Kurus (Arjuna), not by the Vedas, or sacrifices, or study or charity, not even by rites or by rigorous austerities can I be seen in such a form in this world of men by anyone other than you. (48)

Do not be afraid or confused from seeing this horrific form of mine. Now, free from fear and with your mind delighted, behold once more that (familiar) form of mine. (49)

Sanjaya said:

After speaking thus to Arjuna, the son of Vasudeva (Krishna) once more revealed his own (human) form; and assuming again his gentle form, the great spirit consoled the one stricken by fear. (50)

Arjuna said:

O Janardana, having seen your gentle human form, my mind is quieted now and I feel more like my natural self. (51)

The blessed one said:

Very difficult it is to behold this form of mine that you have seen; even the gods are constantly desirous of beholding this form. (52)

Not by the Vedas, nor by austerities, not by charity or by sacrifices can I be seen in this form as you have seen me. (53)

But by unwavering devotion, O Arjuna, can I, in this form, be known and seen in reality; and entered into, O scorcher of the enemies (Arjuna)! (54)

He, who acts for me alone, who makes me his supreme goal, who surrenders himself to me, who is free from attachment, and free from enmity towards any being, O son of Pandu, comes to me. (55)

Philosopher's corner: Chapter analysis and questions for consideration

This is one of the most celebrated chapters of the *Gita* for Hindus as well as non-Hindu religionists and even theoretical physicists. It is claimed that Oppenheimer, the American theoretical physicist, often regarded as the "father of atomic bomb" due to his involvement with the Manhattan project, reportedly recalled that he was reminded of verse 12—"If a thousand suns were to shine forth in the sky all at once, the resulting splendor may be like the brilliance of that great spirit"—while witnessing the first artificial nuclear explosion! Indeed, the images that this chapter invokes are incredibly vivid, striking, terrifying, and awe-inspiring. But how rewarding is this chapter for philosophers?

This chapter offers at least two locations for interesting philosophical engagement. First, it enables us to explore a range of philosophical implications of a direct experience of the divine; and second, it focuses on the role of devotion in our ability to behold the cosmic form of Krishna. In Chapters 9 and 10 Krishna described various dimension and manifestations of his transcendent and immanent nature. At the opening of this chapter Arjuna expresses a desire to "behold"—to have a direct experience—of Krishna's nature. Thus the *Gita* here acknowledges the value of a firsthand account of Krishna's all-pervading immutable self as an important element of the argument meant to convince Arjuna that his worries are misplaced. By allowing such a direct perception of the divine, the *Gita* here also endorses the possibility of a *perception* of the divine and not just a mystical or indirect experience of the divine. Very rarely is the instrumentality of a direct experience of the divine acknowledged in this emphatic fashion. As James in his famous *The Varieties of Religious Experience* writes, "The more concrete objects of most men's religion, the deities whom they worship, are known to them *only in idea*" (James, 1997 (1902), 59 emphasis added). Using the example of Christianity James goes on to write, "the belief in the divine personages" that "determines the prevalent attitude of a believer" is "exerted by the *instrumentality of pure ideas*" (James, 1997 (1902), 59 emphasis added) and not by direct experience. Krishna, however, illustrates a direct perception of the divine here.

It is also interesting what the *Gita* has to say about the elements of such a perception. Since this is a cosmic vision, Arjuna's physical eyes aren't enough; rather, he needs a "divine eye" that Krishna grants him (11.8). Although this chapter does not elaborate on the exact mechanism of this eye, the nature of the cosmic perception might be an interesting question to explore. This might also serve as a point of entry into the discussion of extraordinary and extrasensory perception in many schools of Indian philosophy (e.g., Nyaya). What heighten the drama of this chapter are the nature of Arjuna's encounter and his firsthand reporting of what he witnesses. While Krishna grants this vision to Arjuna, it is not a piecemeal experience where Arjuna has access of a particular episode of Krishna's reality. In its all-pervading nature, this offers an example of one of the boldest of religious experiences.

Further, when Arjuna sees the entire universe united as one in Krishna's body (11.7), the ontological implication of this claim is wide-ranging. Earlier, Krishna has talked about himself as consisting of two natures—the higher nature of the immutable *Brahman* and the lower nature of Prakriti as consisting of the three *gunas* as the location of all actions, agencies, and attachments to egos that result from them. But it wasn't demonstrated how either of these two natures contained the entire universe in its manifest form. In this chapter Krishna offers that verification. So a pertinent question in this regard might be, how this image of an entire universe existing as one in Krishna's "body" fits with the two nature argument? Admittedly, even though Krishna divides the higher nature from the lower nature, he never really makes them into two independent categories as some Hindu schools of philosophy like Samkhya do. However, it is still reasonable to ask how these two parts are united in Krishna's "body" in the cosmic form that Krishna reveals to Arjuna here.

Finally, what makes Krishna reveal himself to Arjuna? Is such a revelation available to others as well and how might one prepare for such a gift? In this infinite form of Krishna, Arjuna sees not only the present, but also what is yet to happen. Krishna not only predicts the outcome that all the heroes will perish but also asserts that they are already killed by him (11.33 and 11.34). What has been the stumbling block for Arjuna is his moral dilemma about how he could fight against and cause the deaths of Drona, Bhishma, and other beloved members of his extended family. Krishna's main strategy has been to neutralize the moral potency of Arjuna's dilemma by exposing the problem in Arjuna's sense of misplaced agency. Arjuna is not causing their deaths—they have already been killed by Krishna. Now what sense can we make of Krishna's agency here especially since he has said earlier (e.g., in 9.9) that none of his actions binds him as he remains unattached? A possible response might be that these heroes are killed by their own past choices/karmas but that would result in a kind of fatalistic determinism that would not be useful for the *Gita's* main argument. Rather than reading and interpreting Krishna's agency in fatalistic terms, it might be useful to read it as a part of Krishna's developing argument in favor of devotion. He pleads with Arjuna to surrender his agency and to perform what his circumstances require as an offering to Krishna. That surrender—the devotion—qualifies one for this vision. As Krishna goes onto say that only "by unwavering devotion" by one "who acts for [him] alone" (11.55) and not by "the Vedas, or sacrifices, or study or charity, not even by rites or by rigorous austerities" (11.48; see also 11.53) can one see Krishna in his divine form. Therefore, it is Krishna's grace that enables this vision. In the process Krishna assumes the agency of all actions thereby bolstering the case for the *yoga* of devotion, which, according to many scholars of the *Gita*, is its predominant *yoga*.

12

The Yoga of Devotion

Summary

This chapter opens with Krishna differentiating between two kinds of seekers: those "who worship what is imperishable, ineffable, unmanifest, all-pervading, inconceivable, immutable, [and] unmoving" and those who worship Krishna. While both reach the same destination of transcending the ocean of "recurring deaths," Krishna's preference seems clearly to be for the latter kind of seekers, those who follow the *yoga* of devotion. Worshipping Krishna is simpler and less arduous for embodied creatures like humans. Further, such a devotee is "extremely dear" to Krishna since in devoting oneself to Krishna an unselfish yogi "does not shrink from the world." Krishna identifies having supreme faith in him as the defining marker for a yogi of devotion. He also differentiates between two kinds of devotees—between "ideal and ordinary" (Malhotra 1999, 45)—thereby offering a nuanced and gradual understanding of being a yogi of devotion.

Arjuna said:

Those devotees who worship you being thus ever disciplined in *yoga*, and those who (worship) the imperishable unmanifest—of these who are better versed in *yoga*? (1)

The blessed one (Krishna) said:

Those who, fixing their minds on me, worship me, remaining ever disciplined in *yoga* (and) being endowed with supreme faith, are in my opinion perfect in *yoga*. (2)

But those who worship the imperishable, the ineffable, the unmanifest, the all-pervading, the inconceivable, the immutable, the immovable, and the ever constant, (3)

Restraining all their senses, with equanimity toward all, they also reach only me, delighting in the welfare of all beings. (4)

It is more arduous for those whose minds are set on the unmanifest; for the path to the unmanifest is hard to attain for embodied beings. (5)

But those who renounce all actions to me, regard me as their supreme goal, worship me by meditating on me with unwavering *yoga*, (6)

For them whose minds are fixed on me, O son of Pritha (Arjuna), I soon arise to rescue them from the ocean of recurring death. (7)

Immerse your mind in me alone, let your understanding enter into me; you will dwell only in me hereafter; of this there is no doubt. (8)

If however you are unable to focus your mind steadily on me, then, O Dhananjaya (Arjuna), seek to attain me by repeated *yoga* practice. (9)

If you are unable even to practice (*yoga*), then act for me by making me your supreme goal; (for) even performing actions for my sake, you will attain perfection. (10)

But if you are unable to do even this, then taking refuge in my *yoga*, relinquish the fruits of all actions with self-mastery. (11)

For knowledge is better than (mere) practice (and) meditation is better than knowledge; the relinquishment of the fruits of action is still better than meditation (because) it brings immediate peace. (12)

One who is free from hatred towards all beings, who is friendly and compassionate; who is unselfish, free from the consciousness of I-ness (egoism), forgiving and even-minded in suffering and joy, (13)

The yogi who is always content, self-controlled, of firm determination, whose mind and understanding are surrendered to me, he is my devotee (and) he is dear to me. (14)

One from whom the world does not shrink and who does not shrink from the world; who is free from exultation, jealousy, fear, and apprehension, he too is dear to me. (15)

He, who is free from expectations, pure (in body and mind), skilled, disinterested, untroubled by circumstances, who has relinquished from initiating (desireful) undertakings, and is devoted to me, he is dear to me. (16)

He, who neither rejoices nor hates, neither grieves nor desires; who has renounced fortune and misfortune, that man of devotion is dear to me. (17)

He, who is the same to foe and friend, and also in honor and disgrace, who is the same in cold and heat, in joy and anguish, (and) is free from attachment, (18)

Equal to blame and praise, one who is quiet and content with whatever comes his way, who is not attached to domesticity, firm in his mind, that man of devotion is dear to me. (19)

But those who cherish this undying *dharma* as I have taught it, intent on me in their faith and making me their supreme goal—such devotees are extremely dear to me. (20)

Philosopher's corner: Chapter analysis and questions for consideration

Part of the reason for Krishna's preference for seekers who follow the *yoga* of devotion is that seeking through worshipping the imperishable is exceedingly difficult to pursue for an embodied being (12.5). The simplicity of the former—with its only requirement of "being endowed with supreme faith" (12.2) in Krishna—appears to be another reason for Krishna's preference. It is also this simplicity that explains the strong hold that this *yoga* has maintained on the hearts and minds of countless Hindus throughout the ages. It is this *yoga* that clearly locates Krishna at the center of the Hindu universe as a personal God that one could relate to.

As I note in the opening Summary to this chapter Krishna discusses two kinds of devotees here. First are those "whose minds are fixed on him" (12.7), who "regard [him] as their supreme goal" (12.6) and who "worship [him] by meditating on [him] with unwavering *yoga*" (12.6). But for those who can't focus their minds steadily on Krishna and are unable to devote themselves to Krishna or make him their ultimate goal (12.9, 12.10, and 12.11), Krishna seems to offer another version of devotion: just take refuge in Krishna and perform every action as an offering and service to Krishna thus relinquishing all the fruits of actions (12.12). In this sense, one becomes a devotee of Krishna by acting "for" him, i.e., "for his sake" (12.10). Acting for Krishna means not acting out of one's own goals and aspirations. The actions of one who has taken refuge in Krishna aren't tainted by thoughts of their intended results. As a result a calm, contented equanimity and even-mindedness ensue in that devotee. Such a balanced and compassionate attitude comes to both kinds of devotees and also to the worshippers of the "imperishable unmanifest." Krishna has introduced and extolled the virtue of equanimity earlier but here elaborates on the multidimensional manifestation of this virtue. Thus this yogi not only sees everything with an equal eye, but is also one "from whom the world does not shrink and who does not shrink from the world" (12.15). A yogi of devotion does not detach oneself from the world; rather, he engages with the world with an attitude of impartiality toward foe and friend as well as an even-mindedness in honor and contempt (12.18).

A few translators (e.g., Easwaran 2007) render the Sanskrit term *bhakti* translated here as "devotion" as "love" and compare the *yoga* of devotion to the way of love of the Christian mystics. In preferring love over knowledge as a path to God, Christian mystics often point to the former's being the safer and surer path and also its ability to light an "ardent fire" to overcome the general weakness of will, often a hindrance in one's spiritual path (Diana Morrison in Easwaran 2007, 205). While the *yoga* of devotion that Krishna proposes here shares elements of commonality with Christian mystics' way of love, it also expands the scope of discussion by highlighting the dimension of equanimity and the unselfish engagement with one's world that it mandates.

From the perspective of comparative moral theory the exact nature of the impartiality implied by equanimity is an interesting topic. Kant emphasizes impartiality while developing the first formulation of his categorical imperative that says "always act in such a way that the maxim of your action can become a universal law." Kant's basic idea is that everyone is equal in the eyes of morality and therefore in order for my action to be considered moral, anyone should be able to act on the motive behind my action. Thus Kant's focus on impartiality is aimed to discount all the particularities of an action, thereby only considering its universal elements in determining its moral worth. Interestingly Krishna's suggestion here seems to be not to discount or overlook ways in which things and circumstances differ, but to engage with them with the mental frame of even-mindedness.

13

The Yoga of Difference between the Field and the Field-Knower

Summary

In this chapter Krishna's focus turns back to issues in ontology and epistemology as he explains the basic categories underlying our reality and knowledge. It also represents a shift in orientation: instead of focusing on Krishna's nature or even on ways of attaining him, this chapter focuses more directly on the nature of the world. This is developed in the context of two sets of distinctions that the *Gita* runs in parallel—between Prakriti and Purusha and between the field and the field-knower.

The early verses introduce some of the categories of Prakriti through which the phenomenal world comes to be furnished with its complexity. The Purusha or the "supreme self" is identified as the "beginningless" "imperishable" principle that exists equally everywhere "as the single sun illumines the entire world." Krishna also elaborates on the nature and object of knowledge that the field-knower possesses. This knowledge liberates one from the cycle of rebirth and it consists of a clear comprehension of the fact that while all actions, all transformations, and changes are modifications of the Prakriti and its constituent *gunas*, the Purusha relates to the phenomenal world as a *mere* "witness." Once one is able to sustain this clear distinction in one's understanding, one's entire attitude and manner of engagement with the world changes. This chapter also provides a sophisticated account of a wide range of dispositions that a field-knower embodies. Characteristics like "unpretentiousness" and "absence of clinging to sons, wives, homes, and the like" are included thereby significantly extending the list beyond the virtue of equanimity emphasized in the previous chapters.

Arjuna said:
O Handsome-haired One, I wish to know (the nature of) Prakriti, Purusha, and also the field and the field-knower, knowledge and that which should be known. (0[1])
The blessed one (Krishna) said:
O son of Kunti (Arjuna), this body is referred to as the "field" (and) one who knows this is called the "field-knower" by those who know him. (1)
O Bharata (Arjuna), also know me to be the field-knower in every field; I deem this knowledge of the field and its knower as true knowledge. (2)
Hear from me briefly about this field, its attributes, its modifications and their causal sources; and also about him (the field-knower) and the nature of his power. (3)
This has been sung in many ways with varied (Vedic) hymns by ancient seers and in the aphorisms about *Brahman*[2] and in their definite reasoned analyses. (4)
The great elements, the sense of I-ness (ego), intellect, and the unmanifest (nature); the ten senses and the one ((inner sense, i.e., mind), and the five sense domains, (5)

Desire, hatred, happiness, suffering, bodily form (that constitutes the basis of) consciousness, persistence—thus is the field with its modifications illustrated in summary. (6)

Humility, unpretentiousness, nonviolence, patience, uprightness, reverence for one's teacher, purity, steadfastness and self-restraint; (7)

Dispassion to the sense-objects and also absence of the sense of I-ness (ego); perception of the defects in birth, death, old age, disease, and suffering; (8)

Nonattachment, absence of clinging to sons, wives, homes, and the like; and constant equanimity of mind in attaining fulfillment and frustration; (9)

Unwavering devotion to me with single-minded *yoga*, retreating to solitary places, having a dislike for a crowd of people; (10)

Constant persistence in the knowledge of the self, perception of the purpose of the knowledge of reality—(all) this is called knowledge; what is contrary to that is ignorance. (11)

(Now) I shall teach you that which is to be known (because) knowing it one attains immortality; (hear about) the beginningless supreme *Brahman* which is said to be neither being nor nonbeing. (12)

With hands and feet (reaching) everywhere, with eyes, mouths and heads (looking) every direction, with (ears) hearing everything, it dwells in the world, enveloping all. (13)

Appearing to have the qualities of all the senses (and yet) being free from all the senses; unattached and yet all supporting; free from the *gunas* and yet enjoying them; (14)

It is outside and within all beings, inanimate and yet animate; incomprehensible because of its subtlety; it is far away yet it is also near. (15)

Undivided, yet remaining as if divided among beings, it is to be known as the supporter of beings and as (their) devourer and generator. (16)

The light of all lights, it is called beyond darkness; knowledge, what is to be known, the goal of all knowing, it is seated in the heart of everyone. (17)

Thus have the field, and also knowledge and the object of knowledge been described in brief; knowing this my devotee enters into my being. (18)

Know that both Prakriti and Purusha are equally beginningless, and know as well that modifications and *gunas* spring from Prakriti. (19)

Prakriti is called the reason for agency, cause and effect; Purusha is called the reason for experiencing joy and suffering. (20)

For Purusha, seated in Prakriti, experiences the *gunas* born of Prakriti; its attachment to the *gunas* is the cause of its births in good and evil wombs. (21)

Witness, consenter, supporter, enjoyer, and the great lord—the supreme Purusha in this body is called the supreme self. (22)

Whoever knows the Purusha, Prakriti along with the *gunas* to be such, is not reborn again—no matter what his current state is. (23)

Through meditation some see the self within the self by the self; others see by the *yoga* of *Samkhya*; still others by the *yoga* of action. (24)

Still others, not knowing thus, worship what they hear from others; they too cross beyond death by being devoted to what they hear. (25)

O bull of the Bharatas (Arjuna), in so far as any being comes into existence—whether stationary or moving—understand that it is born from the union of field and the field-knower. (26)

He (really) sees who sees the highest lord abiding equally in all beings, (and) not perishing when they do. (27)

For seeing the same lord established equally everywhere, he does not injure the self (in others) by the self, (and) thus attains the supreme goal. (28)

And who sees that actions altogether are performed by Prakriti alone and likewise that the self is not an actor, he (truly) sees. (29)

When one perceives diverse states of beings as abiding in the one and their manifestation from that one alone, he then merges with *Brahman*. (30)

O Son of Kunti, because this supreme self is beginningless, free from the *gunas* and imperishable, it does not act nor is defiled (by actions) even though dwelling in a body. (31)

Just as the all-pervading ether is not tainted (by objects it touches) because of its subtlety, so the self, though abiding in every body, is not sullied. (32)

O Bharata, just as the single sun illumines the entire world, so the lord of the field illumines the entire field. (33)

Those who know thus, with the eye of knowledge, the distinction between field and the field-knower, and the freedom of beings from Prakriti, they reach the supreme. (34)

Philosopher's corner: Chapter analysis and questions for consideration

This chapter's offerings for philosophers consist in the areas of ontology and epistemology as it explores the natures of Prakriti, Purusha, *Brahman*, knowledge, and the object of knowledge. While elaborating on Prakriti, Krishna outlines some of the main categories like "great elements, the sense of I-ness (ego) and the intellect" (13.5) through which our familiar world comes to be furnished from the source of Prakriti. Prakriti is also identified as consisting of the three *gunas* which are the sole cause and location for all modifications, episodes, and events in the world (13.29). The three *gunas* and the categories of Prakriti presented here are similar to the categories employed in the Samkhya school of Hindu philosophy as it explains the evolution of the universe. Thus Isvarakrishna provides a detailed account of various evolutes, categories resulting from Prakriti, including the sense of I-ness (*ahamkara*) and the subtle and gross elements, in his third-century text *Samkhya-Karika*, the earliest extant text of this school.

The *Gita* identifies the Purusha as the "supreme self" (13.31), as the "lord of the field" (13.33), as the single principle that is "established equally everywhere" (13.28) and thus as the *Brahman*. While describing the Purusha, Krishna focuses on its all-pervading nature, on its ineffability and incomprehensibility: thus it is depicted as being "outside and within all beings, inanimate and yet animate" and "far away yet ... also near" (13.15). Krishna also goes on to clarify that Purusha is "free from the *gunas*" though it also enjoys them (13.14). Thus it might appear that we get a dualism between Prakriti and Purusha here. However, a comparison with the dualism between Prakriti and Purusha proposed in *Samkhya-Karika* will reveal that the version of dualism we get in the *Gita* is of a much softer kind. Since Samkhya accepts an infinite number of Purushas and do not subsume them under any highest Purusha, it seems very difficult, if not impossible, to embrace Krishna—as he presents himself in the *Gita*—within the Samkhya ontology. Indeed, Samkhya is generally viewed as atheistic due to its rejection of any personal god. Thus, one of the central themes of this chapter, namely, that the highest lord, i.e., Krishna or *Brahman*, abides equally in all beings (13.27), when coupled with Krishna's earlier claim that Prakriti is his lower nature (7.5), turns the dualism between Prakriti and Purusha of the *Gita* into a mere distinction.

Even when conceived as a distinction between Purusha and Prakriti, it might encourage us to think of it in comparison with the most common dualism in Western philosophy, namely, between matter/body and mind (matter being Prakriti and mind being Purusha). However, no such clear comparison is viable. First, because mind is identified as one of the categories evolving out of Prakriti (13.5) and second, because states and attitudes like desire, hatred, happiness, and, above all, consciousness (13.6)—generally associated with the mind in the Western philosophy—are identified as modifications of the "field," i.e., the Prakriti. Thus Prakriti is not only the location of physicality and materiality but also the location and means of agency (13.20), typically associated with the mental realm in the mind-body dualism. One interesting implication of this Prakriti-Purusha dualism, or the matter-Self dualism, is its ability to account for psychophysical causation. The mind-body dualism is often taken to be plagued by its inability to account for cases where we experience a causal interaction between these two realms, as would seem to be a case when *wanting* a cold beverage I *walk* over to the refrigerator to get one. The worry is that if the mental and physical realms are irreducibly distinct as the mind-body dualism proposes then any common causal interaction between the two becomes intractable. The *Gita*, however, avoids this problem since both mentality and physicality and all their causal interactions are located in the realm of Prakriti here.

The need still remains for Krishna to explain how Purusha comes to be associated with Prakriti, i.e., how the self interacts with its embodiment, especially since every being is taken to be "born from the union of field and the field-knower" or the Prakriti and the Purusha (13.26). According to the *Gita* the Purusha is "seated in Prakriti" and thus comes to experience the *gunas* born of Prakriti (13.21). What confuses the Purusha or the self is when it becomes attached to the *gunas* thereby assuming agency of actions that only belongs to the realm of Prakriti. The Purusha in itself is only a "witness" (13.22). Knowledge of this distinction frees one from the cycle of rebirth (13.23). Since it is the habitual attachment of the self to the *gunas* that is taken as the cause of rebirth and bondage, liberatory knowledge comes to be identified with a wide range of dispositions—from that of non-attachment (13.9) and non-violence (13.7) to that of "dislike for a crowd of people" (13.10). Verses 7 through 11 also highlight various properties like "retreating to solitary place" (13.10), "perception of the defects in birth, death, old age, disease, and suffering" (13.8), and attitudes like "dispassion" (13.8), "constant equanimity of mind" (13.9), and "unwavering devotion to Krishna" (13.10) that a knower of this knowledge comes to embody. Thus this could be viewed as the *Gita*'s contribution to the recent discussion in virtue epistemology where various virtues like conscientiousness and open-mindedness that impact a knower's ability are emphasized. Indeed, the vast range of virtues—from uprightness, purity, and absence of clinging to "perception of the purpose of the knowledge of reality" (13.11)—that Krishna endows a person who persists in the knowledge of the self (13.11)—presents a comprehensive list that includes both intellectual and moral virtues.

Finally, expounding on the nature of this knowledge, Krishna argues that a person with the knowledge of this supreme self "*sees* that actions altogether are performed by Prakriti alone and likewise that the self is not an actor" (13.29, emphasis added). What kind of activity is implied in this "seeing" though? How is this seeing and "perceiving" (13.30) different from ordinary examples of seeing, for example, when I see the teapot on the table? Krishna also offers an argument by analogy, which is popular in Indian philosophy, when he says, "Just as the all-pervading ether in not tainted (by objects it touches) because of its subtlety, so the self, though abiding in every body, is not sullied" (13.32). But it is interesting to explore whether this analogy has the strength to deliver us at Krishna's intended conclusion that even though the self is in the body, it is not touched by the body and its modifications.

Notes

1 While some versions of the *Gita* don't include this verse, many others do. I have decided to include it since it frames Krishna's response to Arjuna in this chapter nicely.

2 Ramanuja in his *Gita Bhasya* interprets the term "brahma sutra" in this verse to refer to *Brahma-sutra*, a text credited to Bādarāyaṇa, considered fundamental in the Vedanta schools of Hindu philosophy (Adidevananda 2009, 430). While some later interpreters of the *Gita* follow this interpretation, others find it rather "improbable that this work [*Brahma-sutra*] existed in the time of the Gita" (Edgerton 1972, 99).

14

The Yoga of the Division of Three *Gunas*

Summary

This chapter offers a detailed description of the three *gunas*, namely, goodness, passion, and dark inertia—the constituents of Prakriti—that "imprison the imperishable embodied self in the body" by undergirding all its attachments. In so doing their interactions create the multifariousness of our phenomenal reality. Such diversity is explained along two axes. The first axis defines each *guna* in terms of its associated character traits and behavioral dispositions. For example, goodness "being untainted" is associated with the disposition or propensity to happiness and knowledge. The second axis maintains that a person's overall character is determined in terms of one *guna* being predominant in one's nature over the other two. More specifically it outlines how such a predominance is reflected in a person's behaviors and dispositions. Thus, if goodness is predominant over passion and dark inertia in one's nature then that person is naturally disposed to happiness and knowledge. This chapter also offers an ontological foundation for the virtue of equanimity since a yogi with equanimity is always cognizant that *only* the *gunas* act and thus is able to remain undisturbed—"unmoved"—in pleasure and pain or "honor and insult." Krishna concludes the chapter by reiterating that the "undeviating" *yoga* of devotion allows one to transcend the three *guna*s.

The blessed one (Krishna) said:

I shall declare again the highest knowledge that transcends all knowledge; knowing which, all the sages have gone from this world to supreme perfection. (1)

Having resorted to this knowledge, they come to identify with my *dharma*; they are not born even at the time of world creation, nor do they suffer any sorrow at the time of dissolution. (2)

My womb is the great *Brahman*, in which I place the embryo; from this, O Bharata (Arjuna), comes the origin of all beings. (3)

O son of Kunti (Arjuna), whatever forms are produced in all wombs, *Brahman* is their great womb, (and) I am the seed-giving father. (4)

O mighty-armed (Arjuna)! Goodness, passion and dark inertia—the three *guna*s born of Prakriti imprison the imperishable embodied self in the body. (5)

O sinless one (Arjuna), of these, goodness, being untainted, is illuminating and healthy; (yet) it binds one by (creating) attachment to happiness and to knowledge. (6)

O son of Kunti, know that passion is of the disposition of desire, born of thirst and attachment; it binds the embodied one by attachment to action. (7)

But, O Bharata, know that dark inertia born of ignorance confuses every embodied self; it binds one by negligence, laziness, and slumber. (8)

O Bharata, goodness brings about attachment to happiness, passion to actions; however, dark inertia, veiling knowledge, brings about attachment to negligence. (9)

O Bharata, sometimes goodness prevails, overpowering passion and dark inertia; sometimes passion (prevails, overpowering) goodness and dark inertia and likewise dark inertia (prevails, obscuring) goodness and passion. (10)

When the light of knowledge shines through all the (sense) gates of this body, then also one should know that goodness is prevalent. (11)

O bull of the Bharatas (Arjuna), predominance of passion causes greed, activity, the undertaking of actions, restlessness and longing. (12)

O joy of the Kurus (Arjuna), predominance of dark inertia causes lack of illumination and inactivity, negligence and mere delusion. (13)

But if the embodied one dies when goodness is prevalent, then he enters the untainted worlds of those who know the highest. (14)

Dying in passion (i.e., when passion is prevalent), one is reborn among those attached to action; likewise, dying in dark inertia (i.e., when dark inertia is prevalent), one is reborn into deluded wombs. (15)

The fruit of action well performed, they say, is pure and of the nature of goodness; but the fruit of passion is suffering (and) ignorance is the fruit of dark inertia. (16)

From goodness knowledge is born, from passion only greed; and from dark inertia come carelessness, delusion, and also ignorance. (17)

Those who are established in goodness go upward; those who are established in passion dwell in the middle; those of dark inertia, abiding in the scope of the lowest *guna*, sink low. (18)

When a person of vision sees no agent except the (three) *guna*s, and knows that which is higher than the *guna*s, he enters into my being. (19)

Transcending these three *guna*s—the cause of embodiment—the embodied one attains immortality, being freed from birth, death, old age, and suffering. (20)

Arjuna said:

O lord! By what signs is one marked who passes beyond the three *guna*s? How does he behave? And, how are these three *guna*s transcended? (21)

The blessed one said:

O son of Pandu (Arjuna), he does not hate illumination or activity or even delusion when they arise, nor does he long (after them) when they have ceased. (22)

Who sits as if disinterested, unmoved by the *guna*s; who remains firm and unwavering thinking "only gunas are in motion;" (23)

To whom joy and suffering are the same, who is established in himself, to whom a lump of clay, stone, or gold are the same; the steadfast man, to whom the pleasant and unpleasant are equal, to whom blame and praise to himself are equal; (24)

Equal to honor and insult, equal to the sides of friend and foe, abandoning all undertakings—he is said to have transcended the *guna*s. (25)

And he who serves me with undeviating *yoga* of devotion; transcending these *guna*s, he is fit to be absorbed in *Brahman*. (26)

For I am the foundation of *Brahman*, the immortal and immutable; and the basis of eternal *dharma* and of perfect bliss. (27)

Philosopher's corner: Chapter analysis and questions for consideration

In previous chapters Krishna has identified *Brahman* with the Purusha and also with his higher nature (see, for example, 13.12, 13.14, and 13.30). In this chapter he identifies the *Brahman* as his "great womb" and himself as the "seed-giving father" (14.4). From this it appears that this *Brahman* is more like the Prakriti than the Purusha. So there seems to be an inconsistency in Krishna's account of the nature of *Brahman*. The following points help us shed some light on this apparent inconsistency and any worries that it might pose for Krishna's overall project. First, the ultimate goal of the *Gita* is to present Krishna as the most fundamental ontological concept. Thus the Upanishadic concept of *Brahman* as the ultimate reality gets subsumed under Krishna here. Early on in the *Gita* Krishna introduces the distinction between his higher nature and lower nature as a way to elucidate the ontological framework underlying our universe, our phenomenal experience as well as our ultimate liberation from cycles of rebirth. Further, the dualism between Prakriti and Purusha that ensues in the *Gita* functions as a methodological dualism where the dualism is used to illuminate a point but not to be ultimately embraced as irreducible. It is methodological since the *Gita* is not interested in the dualism per se but only in so far as it highlights the point that liberation consists of transcending the *gunas* achieved with undeviating *yoga* of devotion to Krishna (14.26). Thus since Purusha and Prakriti are two aspects of Krishna's same nature, it doesn't seem as problematic to have *Brahman*—which is often equated with Krishna in the *Gita*—be identified with Purusha and Prakriti on different occasions. In the light of this analysis it makes sense when Krishna says that transcending the *gunas*, a yogi becomes "fit to be absorbed in the *Brahman*" (14.26), or that he is the "foundation of *Brahman*" (14.27).

In providing a detailed account of the three *gunas* of goodness, passion, and dark inertia, in this chapter Krishna introduces a way to understand the natural hierarchy among people in terms of the *guna* that is predominant or prevalent in their nature. This discussion thus becomes important in relation to the *Gita*'s contribution in the area of social philosophy. Earlier chapters of the *Gita* emphasized the sameness that exists in all beings through championing the idea that the same self/*Brahman*/Krishna exists in all of us just as the single sun illuminates the entire world (see, for example, 13.32). The emphasis of this chapter, however, is different, and instead works to provide an explanation for the wide range of diversity among people and the underlying mechanism through which people come of have different talents, aptitudes, and temperaments which designate them to different castes or social classes, as the final chapter of the *Gita* will argue. The three *gunas* are proclaimed to be the "cause of embodiment" (14.20) and thus to provide the material substance of our universe by constituting Prakriti. But unlike other purely material principles, the Prakriti and its *gunas* also make up the mental faculties. The most prominent characteristic of these *gunas* is their efficacy in giving rise to certain dispositions, attitudes, and strong behavioral tendencies. As Krishna writes, "goodness brings about attachment to happiness, passion to actions" and "dark inertia, veiling knowledge, brings about attachment to negligence" (14.9). Given this variety in associated dispositions, one's dominant character traits give evidence to the predominance of one *guna* over the other two in her nature. Thus predominance of goodness causes keenness for knowledge (14.11) and what has been termed "the sattvafication" that is deemed crucial in the path to liberation by the

Samkhya and Yoga schools of Hindu philosophy (see, for example, Phillips 2009, 280; see also 14.14). Predominance of passions, on the other hand, causes greed, activity, and longing, among other things (14.12) and predominance of dark inertia causes inactivity, negligence, and delusion, among others (14.13). Further, according to Krishna, people of goodness "go upward," people of passion "dwell in the middle," and people of dark inertia "sink low" (14.18). While these directional movements need not be read exclusively in social terms, their implication for discussion in social philosophy should not be underestimated.

The impact of these *gunas* is not limited to the present lifetime of an individual but reaches over to the next life as well. As Krishna clarifies, the *guna* that is prevalent at the time of death of an individual determines her next station. For example, if passion is prevalent, the person "is reborn among those attached to action" and if dark inertia is prevalent, the person "is reborn into the wombs of delusion" (14.15). Especially if we take this claim in the light of karma theory, the exact mechanism of this determination is an interesting question to pursue. Further, is the mechanism same as the one Krishna alluded to in Chapter 8 while stating, "whatever state of being a man remembers while leaving his body at the time of death, to that state alone he enters due to his ever persistence in it" (8.6)? Additionally, since these *gunas* are not of the nature that they can be perceived directly, the exact nature of any evidentiary support for this theory of determination of human nature also becomes an interesting question. Finally, when Krishna describes a person who "passes beyond the three *gunas*" (14.21) as one who "does not hate illumination or activity or even delusion when they arise, nor does he long (after them) when they have ceased" (14.22) thus remaining "unmoved by the *gunas*" (14.23), his characterization seems to resemble the Buddhist principle of mindfulness, where the goal is to focus on every arising state and emotion without becoming attached to them or acting on their impulsions. Harry Frankfurt's (1971) distinction between first-order desires and second-order desires—between, for example, my desire to learn how to swim and my desire to desire to learn how to swim—could also be used here to interpret the distinction that

Krishna has in mind. A yogi notices the first-order desires and other arisings in her mind without thereby having the associated second-order desire to act upon them.[1]

Note

1 Thanks to Stephen Phillips for drawing my attention to this point.

15

The Yoga of the Supreme Purusha

Summary

This short chapter offers a summary of some of the main philosophical themes from the last several chapters: Krishna is identified with the "primeval Purusha" and his "supreme abode" is identified as the destination from which there is no return into the realm of births and rebirths. The phenomenal world is identified as the realm of Prakriti where all actions are located. It uses the image of an upside-down ashvattha, or peepal tree, to capture our intimate entanglements with our phenomenal reality and to depict the goal of liberation in terms of cutting down this strong-rooted tree "with the powerful axe of non-attachment." This chapter outlines three Purushas—the destructible or the ego selves that ensue from Prakriti, the indestructible or the "fragment" of Krishna that becomes "the eternal essence of life," and, finally, the "highest Purusha," the supreme self that lies beyond the first two. In so doing Krishna offers himself as the foundational ontological category where all the various concepts introduced to explain our world hang together.

The blessed one (Krishna) said:

They (the wise) speak of an eternal ashvattha (peepal) tree, with its roots above and branches under, and whose leaves are (Vedic) hymns; He who knows it knows the Vedas. (1)

Its branches spread out below and above, nourished by the *gunas*, with sense-objects as sprouts; and below, into the world of men, extend its (aerial) roots engendering action. (2)

Its form is not thus understood here in the world, nor its end or beginning or its extent; having cut down this strong-rooted ashvattha (peepal) tree with the powerful axe of non-attachment, (3)

Then that realm must be sought after, which upon reaching they don't return from, (with this thought): "I take refuge in that same primeval Purusha, from whom issued forth the primordial (entire cosmic) activity." (4)

Without pride or delusion, the fault of attachment conquered, ever intent on the self within, their desires ceased, freed from the dualities known as pleasure and pain, undeluded men go to that realm beyond change. (5)

Neither the sun, nor the moon nor fire illumines that, my supreme abode; having gone to which they do not return. (6)

Only a fragment of me in the living world becomes the eternal essence of life; it pulls along the (five) senses including the mind as the sixth, that abide in Prakriti. (7)

When the lord (as the embodied self) acquires a body and also when he leaves it, he takes these (the senses and the mind) along, even as the wind wafts away scents from their source. (8)

Presiding over hearing, sight, and touch, taste, and smell, along with mind, he savors the objects of the senses. (9)

Deluded men do not perceive him as he leaves (the body) or remains (in the body), or enjoys (sense objects) through contacts with the *gunas*; (but) those with the eyes of knowledge perceive him. (10)

The yogis who strive, see him present in themselves; but those who are undisciplined and of unrefined minds fail to see him even when they strive. (11)

The brilliance of the sun that illumines the whole universe, and that (light) which is in the moon and in fire—know that radiance to be mine. (12)

And entering into the earth I sustain all beings by my strength; and I nourish all herbs having become Soma, the liquid of moonlight. (13)

Having become Vaishvanara (digestive, fiery power), I exist within the body of (all) living beings; acting through the flow of vital breath I digest four kinds of food. (14)

Also, I dwell deep in the heart of all beings and from me come memory, knowledge and the dispelling (of doubt); indeed, I am that which is to be known through all the Vedas; and I am their knower and the creator of the Vedanta (their final truth). (15)

There are two Purushas in the world, the destructible and the indestructible; the destructible is all beings, the indestructible is called "sublime, at the summit of existence." (16)

But there exists a highest Purusha, other than these, designated as the supreme self; the immutable lord who, entering into the three worlds, sustains them. (17)

Since I am beyond the destructible and am also higher than the indestructible, therefore, I am celebrated as the supreme Purusha in the world and in the Vedas. (18)

One, who knows me without delusion thus as the supreme Purusha, he knows all; O Bharata (Arjuna)! he worships me with his whole being. (19)

Herewith, O sinless one (Arjuna), I have taught you this most secret tradition; realizing it, a man acquires understanding and becomes one who has successfully fulfilled all his duties, O Bharata! (20)

Philosopher's corner: Chapter analysis and questions for consideration

The chapter opens with the imagery of an eternal ashvattha tree to represent our phenomenal world. The ashvattha (peepal) tree is considered sacred by a number of religions in South East Asia, including Hinduism and Buddhism. In 10.26 Krishna identified himself as the ashvattha, the best among trees. In the opening verse of this chapter he draws upon the idea of the ashvattha tree to symbolically represent our phenomenal world. Krishna claims that this tree has its "roots above" and branches below (15.1) and that its roots extend "into the world of men" "engendering action" and that it is "nourished by the *gunas*" (15.2). In relation to this counterintuitive idea of having the roots above, most commentators of the *Gita* point to the fact that since the tree is taken to symbolize our phenomenal world and roots are taken to be the source from which the world follows, so it makes sense that they are taken to be up above. As Ramanuja, a Vedanta philosopher of medieval India, writes in his commentary of this verse, this ashvattha tree has "its roots above since it has its roots in Brahma who is seated above the seven worlds. It has 'branches below' ending with denizens like men, animals, beasts, worms, insects, birds and immovable" (Adidevananda 2009, 484). I want to offer another possible significance of this tree having its roots above. Typically the roots of a tree remain out of our everyday vision. Roots also hold a tree in place anchoring it. That is how this tree representing the phenomenal world appears to most people. However, Krishna also assures that this tree has its roots right in front of us and thus not hidden from us even though we ordinarily fail to see the roots and how they come to entangle us. Thus Krishna's advice is to "cut down this strong-rooted ashvattha tree with the powerful axe of nonattachment" (15.3).

In this chapter Krishna also consolidates various claims made so far in relation to the nature of Purusha into a classification of three Purushas. Thus he identifies two Purushas in the world (15.16): the "destructible" (or Prakriti) and the "indestructible" or his immutable higher nature providing the essence of life. But Krishna goes on to identify yet another level of Purusha—the "supreme Purusha" (15.18), the "supreme self" (15.17)—that is beyond both the destructible and the indestructible Purushas. He could be taken to be making the further argument that the distinction between these two is viable only from the perspective of a person who is ignorant of Krishna's true nature. One who knows Krishna as the supreme Purusha knows him "without delusion" and such a person worships Krishna "with his whole being" (15.19). Thus while all the classifications among various Purushas and Krishna's various natures are useful for the purpose of explaining how the phenomenal reality ensues from Krishna's nature, they seem to dissolve in Krishna's final analysis. This chapter also contributes to the nature of synthesis that many commentators of the *Gita* take it to offer between various strands of Hinduism by clearly incorporating the Vedas and the Vedanta within its purview.

16

The Yoga of the Division between the Divine and the Demonic

Summary

This chapter focuses on outlining the natures of two kinds of beings—divine and demonic—as reflected in their associated traits. Divine traits include nonviolence, truth, and gentleness, while demonic traits include vanity, arrogance, hypocrisy, and "intoxication of wealth." Since divine traits are discussed in previous chapters, Krishna's focus in this chapter is on providing an elaborate list of the demonic traits. These traits depict the demonic person to be a skeptic in believing that "the world has no truth," an atheist in maintaining that the world has "no god," and a hedonist in arguing that the sole purpose of life is the "fulfillment of their desires." Most importantly, a demonic person acts from an all-engulfing egotism. While divine traits lead to liberation from the cycle of rebirth, demonic traits lead to the worst kind of bondage, namely, to a seemingly endless lifetimes in hell. Thus, "lust, anger, and greed"—three more prominent demonic traits—are described as the "three doors to hell" or "three gates to darkness."

The blessed one (Krishna) said:

Fearlessness, purity of heart, constant perseverance in the *yoga* of knowledge, charity, subjugation (of the senses), sacrifice, study of the scriptures, austerity, uprightness; (1)

Nonviolence, truth, absence of anger, renunciation, peace, nonslanderousness, compassion towards all beings, absence of greed, gentleness, modesty, lack of restlessness; (2)

Brilliance, forgiveness, resolve, cleanliness, freedom from the sense of enmity, absence of pride; these are the traits of one born with the divine nature, O Bharata (Arjuna). (3)

O son of Pritha (Arjuna), hypocrisy, arrogance, excessive pride, anger, and also harshness (in speech) and ignorance; these are the traits of one with the demonic nature. (4)

The divine traits are deemed to lead to liberation, the demonic ones to bondage; do not despair, O son of Pandu (Arjuna), you were born with the divine. (5)

There are two (kinds of) beings created in this world: the divine and the demonic; I described the divine at length, now hear from me of the demonic, O son of Pritha. (6)

Demonic men don't know the right path of action or when to refrain from action; there exists neither cleanliness, nor even proper conduct, nor truth in them. (7)

They say, "the world has no truth, no foundation, no god; (it is) not produced by the power of mutual dependence, its sole purpose is desire—what else?" (8)

Holding fast to this view, these ruined men of meager understanding rise up as enemies, committing terrible acts for the destruction of the world. (9)

Clinging to insatiable desire, being drunk with pride and hypocrisy, possessing false notions from delusion, they act with impure resolve. (10)

Clinging to immeasurable anxiety that ends only with death, they think that fulfillment of their desires is the highest goal and are certain that that is all. (11)

Bound by a hundred fetters of hope and expectation, enslaved by desire and anger, they strive to amass wealth dishonestly for the gratification of their desires. (12)

"I have acquired this wish today, now I shall satisfy that one; this wealth is mine, and more shall also be mine;" (13)

"I have killed this enemy and I will slay others too; I am the lord, I am the enjoyer, I am successful, strong, and happy." (14)

"I am rich and well-born; who else is equal to me? I shall sacrifice, give (gifts), and rejoice," thus they speak, deluded by ignorance. (15)

Confused by endless fancy, ensnared by the web of delusion, addicted to satisfying their desires, they sink into a foul hell. (16)

Self-aggrandizing, stubborn, filled with pride and intoxication of wealth, they sacrifice in name only, in hypocrisy, and without following the scriptural norms. (17)

Resorting to egotism, force, arrogance, desire, and anger, these envious men hate me in their own bodies as in others'. (18)

Again and again I cast these cruel, hateful, vile, and impure men into the cycles of rebirth (and) into demonic wombs alone. (19)

Falling into a demonic womb, deluded in birth after birth, they fail to ever attain me; O son of Kunti (Arjuna), they thus descend to the lowest depths. (20)

Lust, anger, and greed—these constitute this threefold gate of hell that destroys the self; therefore, one must renounce these three. (21)

O son of Kunti, being liberated from these three gates of darkness, a man performs what is good for the self and therefore reaches the highest goal. (22)

He who forsakes the scriptural norms and lives to fulfill his (selfish) desires, he does not attain perfection, nor happiness, nor the highest goal. (23)

Therefore, let the scriptures be your standard in determining what to do or to avoid; knowing what is enjoined in the norms of the scriptures, you should perform (those) actions in this world. (24)

Philosopher's corner: Chapter analysis and questions for consideration

Earlier in the *Gita*, Krishna emphasized the need to cultivate many of the divine traits—for example, non-violence, compassion, and forgiveness—through the practice of various *yoga*s. However, in this chapter Krishna's focus is on the demonic traits and how a person comes to be endowed with them (or the divine traits) by being placed into a certain kind of womb. Krishna informs Arjuna that he casts people of demonic traits into demonic wombs again and again through cycles of rebirths (16.19). Krishna assures Arjuna that he has nothing to worry as he was "born with the divine" traits (16.5; see also 16.3) presumably given his noble birth. But can this argument be viable in a non-Hindu context?

What marks the lists of divine and demonic traits is the wide range within each list. Among the list of traits associated with the divine nature Krishna highlights fearlessness, purity of heart, charity (16.1), and cleanliness (16.3). While some of these traits are self-regarding, in being focused on one's attitude toward aspects of oneself, like "subjugation (of the senses)" (16.1), "modesty," and "lack of restlessness" (16.2), other divine traits on Krishna's list are clearly other-regarding in the sense that in their expression attitudes toward others are included. Thus, "compassion towards all beings" (16.2) and "freedom from the sense of enmity" (16.3) are other-regarding. Similarly, the list of demonic traits includes traits marked by moral failing: for example, of "hypocrisy," "arrogance," and "excessive pride" (16.4); but the list also includes general intellectual shortcomings like "ignorance" (16.4), confusion and wrong views (16.7, 16.10, and 16.16). More specifically, the demonic traits are marked by their adherence to false doctrines according to Krishna. Thus people of demonic traits think: "the world has no truth, no foundation, no god; (it is) not produced by the power of mutual dependence, its sole purpose is desire" (16.8). Here Krishna seems to acknowledge the popularity of the Carvaka, the materialist school of Indian philosophy, that championed a starkly anti-Vedic perspective that not only denied the possibility of afterlife or rebirth or the karma theory, but was also hedonistic in its moral outlook in its focus on "gratification of desire" (16.12) as the goal of human life. According to Krishna, people of demonic nature "rise up as enemies, committing terrible acts for the destruction of the world" (16.9). Their principal offense is against the moral order of the world envisioned in the *Gita*. How exactly do they engender the destruction of the world by having false convictions? Presumably they become "enemies" by subscribing to and professing wrong and potentially dangerous views.

An interesting question to ask in this regard: what is a person of demonic nature guilty of either morally or intellectually? In the context of Western ethical sensibilities, generally speaking an action is wrong or immoral if it fails to fulfill the requirements of a standard of morality. Often a wrong act is one that is injurious and harmful to oneself and others. But when Krishna portrays a demonic person as thinking, "I am rich and well-born; who else is equal to me? I shall sacrifice, give (gifts), and rejoice" (16.15), it remains unclear what this person's exact moral or intellectual offense is. Krishna identifies "lust, anger and greed" as the "threefold gate of hell" (16.21). The central problem with demonic traits is that they lead to bondage and thus result in people with these traits being "cast again and again into demonic wombs through cycles of rebirth" (16.19) by Krishna. Once again one might wonder what might be the value of Krishna's discussion of demonic traits, especially in a non-Hindu philosophical context. In developing the contrast between the divine and demonic traits in stark and clear opposition here, Krishna seems to be underplaying the roles of moderation and cultivation in his overall message. So can we still consider one of the dominant moral strands of the *Gita* to be of virtue ethics that seems to focus on the cultivation of moderation? An interesting exercise from the perspective of comparative ethics might be to consider all the different traits Krishna lists and evaluate their appropriateness for being considered right or wrong.

17

The Yoga of the Threefold Faith

Summary

In Chapter 14 Krishna offered a detailed account of the three *guna*s of goodness, passion, and dark inertia that constitute Prakriti and in turn provide the material ingredients of our phenomenal world. Krishna had also elaborated on the behavioral and dispositional counterparts for the different *guna*s. In the present chapter he aligns them with threefold divisions in faith, food, sacrifice, austerity, and charity. In each dimension goodness is reflected in acts that promote longevity, health, and happiness and are in accordance with scriptural norms; passion is reflected in acts that cause pain and sorrow and are done in the hope of a reward; and dark inertia is reflected in acts that violate scriptural norms and cause self-mortification or "destruction of others." The chapter concludes with an analysis of the Sanskrit mantra "OM-TAT-SAT" and the statement that every seeker of liberation starts their acts of sacrifice, charity, and austerity with this sacred chant.

Arjuna said:

Men who neglect the scriptural norms but perform sacrifices filled with faith, O Krishna, what condition is basic in them—goodness, passion, or dark inertia? (1)

The blessed one (Krishna) said:

Threefold is the faith of the embodied selves born of their nature—characterized by goodness, passion or dark inertia. Hear about it! (2)

O Bharata (Arjuna), the faith of each person is in agreement with his inborn nature; man is made up of faith; as his faith is, so indeed is he. (3)

Men of goodness worship the gods, men of passion the demigods and demons; the others, men of dark inertia, offer worship to ghosts and hordes of goblins. (4)

Those who perform terrible austerities not enjoined by the scriptural norms, being trapped in hypocrisy and egotism, and filled with desire, passion and force, (5)

Mindlessly, they torment the elements in their bodies and me as well residing within the body; know that they have the demonic resolve. (6)

But food that is dear to everyone is also of three kinds; so also are their sacrifices, austerities and charity; hear now about the distinction between them. (7)

Foods that promote longevity, energy, strength, health, happiness and cheerfulness, and that are savory, smooth, firm and agreeable are dear to the men of goodness. (8)

Foods that are bitter, sour, salty, excessively hot, pungent, dry, and burning, and that cause pain, sorrow and sickness are preferred by men of passion. (9)

Foods that are stale, insipid, putrid, spoiled, left over and impure are enjoyed by the men of dark inertia. (10)

A sacrifice is of the nature of goodness when it is offered without any desire for the fruit, in accordance with scriptural norms, and with the mental resolve that it has to be performed simply (for its own sake). (11)

But when a sacrifice is performed in the hope of a reward and for the sake of mere hypocritical show, O best of the Bharatas (Arjuna), know that to be of the nature of passion. (12)

A sacrifice is declared to be of the nature of dark inertia when it violates the scriptural norms, in which no ritual food offering is distributed, nor any chants recited or gifts given to the priest; (and) which is devoid of faith. (13)

Honoring of gods, the twice-borns (members of the Brahmin caste), teachers and the wise; and (practicing) purity, honesty, celibacy and nonviolence are called austerity of the body. (14)

Uttering words that cause no agitation, and that are truthful, pleasant and beneficial, and also daily recitations of the Vedas are called the austerity of the speech. (15)

Mental serenity, gentleness, silence, self-control, and purity of being are called austerity of the mind. (16)

This threefold austerity is declared to be of the nature of goodness when persevering men perform it with highest faith and without desiring any fruit. (17)

Austerities practiced for gaining recognition, honor and reverence and with mere hypocrisy are called in this world to be of the nature of passion; they are unstable and fleeting. (18)

Austerities performed with deluded perception, self-mortification, or for the destruction of others are declared to be of the nature of dark inertia. (19)

When a charitable donation is made for the sake of duty alone, given at a proper time and place to a deserving recipient who cannot (return) the favor—that is thought to be of the nature of goodness. (20)

But when a charity is offered to secure some favor in return, or again in expectation of a future reward, or with reluctance—that is thought to be of the nature of passion. (21)

Charity given at the wrong place and wrong time, and to an unworthy recipient, without proper regard and with contempt, is declared to be of the nature of dark inertia. (22)

"OM-TAT-SAT" ("That Is the Real") is said to be the triple designation of *Brahman* that gave primordial sanctity to the brahmins (members of the priest caste), the Vedas and sacrifice. (23)

Therefore the knowers of the *Brahman* start their every act of sacrifice, charity, and austerity prescribed by the scriptures with the chant of "OM." (24)

With the word "TAT" ("That") and without desiring fruits the seekers of liberation perform acts of sacrifice and austerity, and various acts of charity. (25)

O son of Pritha (Arjuna), the word "SAT" is used with the meaning of reality and the meaning of goodness; this word is also used for an action that merits spiritual praise. (26)

The Steadfastness in sacrifice, austerity and charity is also spoken of as "SAT"; likewise, any action for these purposes is also denoted by "SAT" ("Good"). (27)

But, O son of Pritha, whatever oblation or charity is offered, whatever austerity is practiced or action is performed without faith is called "ASAT" ("Untrue"), and has no meaning here or in the world after death. (28)

Philosopher's corner: Chapter analysis and questions for consideration

Krishna opens this chapter by characterizing three kinds of people according to the food of their preference. For example, people of goodness are claimed to enjoy "savory, smooth, [and] firm" "foods that promote longevity, energy, strength, health, happiness and cheerfulness" (17.8); people of passion enjoy "bitter, sour, salty and excessively hot" food that cause pain and sickness (17.9); and people of dark inertia enjoy food that is "stale, insipid, putrid, spoiled, left over and impure" (17.10). In a similar fashion Krishna clarifies that if a sacrifice, austerity or charity is done for its own sake or done selflessly, then it is of the nature of goodness (17.11); if it is done "in the hope of a reward and for the sake of mere hypocritical show" (17.12), then it is of the nature of passion; and if the action "violates the scriptural norms" (17.13) and are for "self-mortification" or for injuring others (17.19), then they are considered of the nature of dark inertia.

The focus of the chapter, however, is on threefold faith as Krishna takes a person's faith to be "in agreement with his inborn nature" (17.3). In discussions of faith in the context of Western philosophy what is often emphasized is its distinction from reason and its epistemological and argumentative imports. It is also commonly assumed that faith is a matter of choice and more specifically it is a decision to believe in something without necessarily having a complete or sufficient rational support. Krishna's claim, "man is made up of faith; as his faith is, so indeed is he" (17.3), on the other hand, seems to draw a very different picture. Faith here is no longer a matter of choice which can be suspended at will but is aligned with the very natural and dispositional constituents of one's nature. It is important to note here that the Sanskrit term *shraddha*, which is translated here as "faith," refers to a semantic range of concepts that includes awareness, complete dedication, and surrender, and such a range is not typically captured by the English term "faith." Thus the *Gita*'s use of the term "faith" here is far broader than our common Western meaning since the *Gita* not only accommodates different correlated dispositions of faith, but also elaborates on how they are expressed in one's preference for food, and aptitude for performances of sacrifice and austerities. A question to explore in this comparative context is whether the term "faith" is used with overlapping meanings in these two contexts. It appears that for the *Gita* faith is not just a matter of belief, but a core determinant of our very beings. How useful might this way of thinking about faith be for our contemporary sensibilities?

When Krishna characterizes a charitable donation that is "made for the sake of duty alone" (17.20) as a charity that is of the nature of goodness, he provides us with a very concrete context of comparison with Kant's theory of the categorical imperative. While their unmistakable similarity cannot be overlooked since like Kant, Krishna here counsels to perform one's duty "for the sake of duty," it remains an open question how the latter part of this verse might fit in a Kantian framework of categorical imperatives. Thus when Krishna says, "given at proper time and place to a deserving recipient who cannot (return) the favor" (17.20), is he aiming for impartiality? Further, even so, is this impartiality mediated through mere universalizability? While these acts of charitable donation do seem to be "from duty" and not just "in accordance with duty," their exact import for impartiality, a cornerstone of the Kantian moral project remains unclear. Verses 23 through 28 have relevance from the perspective of philosophy of language especially since a linguistic entity ("OM-TAT-SAT") is taken here not just to allow us to describe a reality but also to embody the force, power, and knowledge of that reality.

18

The Yoga of Liberation and Renunciation

Summary

This final chapter is one of the two longest teachings of the *Gita* partly because Krishna can be interpreted here as attempting a systematic synthesis of various strands of his main argument that he developed in different chapters. As a corollary of the three *gunas* introduced earlier, here Krishna extends his discussion of the three dimensions in everything we humans engage in, namely, in our knowing, relinquishing of fruits of actions, agencies, understanding, resolve and happiness, and clarifies that they can be of the nature of goodness, or of passion, or of dark inertia. He identifies five causes implied in any action. Krishna also enumerates the duties of members of the four castes that are born of the *guna* distribution in their respective nature and extolls the supreme efficacy of the *yoga* of devotion in realizing the dual goal of freedom from the cycle of rebirth and becoming one with Krishna. Krishna's arguments are successful as the chapter concludes with Arjuna's statement that his "delusion is destroyed" and that he "regained memory (i.e. understanding)" by Krishna's grace, and finally that he stood firm, ready to act in accordance with Krishna's command.

Arjuna said:

O Hrishikesha, O Mighty-armed, O Slayer of Demon Keshi! I desire to know the true meaning of renunciation and of relinquishment and the distinction between them. (1)

The blessed one (Krishna) said:

Sages understand the giving up of actions done with desire as "renunciation"; the wise declare the surrendering of all fruits of actions as "relinquishment." (2)

"All action should be forsaken as they are flawed": so say some wise; but others say action such as sacrifice, charity and austerity ought not to be abandoned. (3)

O best of the Bharatas (Arjuna), hear my decision about relinquishment; for relinquishment has been declared to be of three kinds, O tiger among men (Arjuna)! (4)

The acts of sacrifice, charity and austerity should not be relinquished but surely performed, for they—sacrifice, charity and austerity, purify the wise. (5)

But even these actions should be performed, O son of Pritha (Arjuna), by relinquishing attachments to them and the desire for their fruits—this is my supreme and sure conviction. (6)

But the renunciation of prescribed action is inappropriate; relinquishment of such action out of delusion is declared to be of the nature of dark inertia. (7)

One who relinquishes an action as being painful, for fear of bodily harm—his relinquishment is of the nature of passion; he cannot even win the fruit of relinquishment. (8)

O Arjuna, when one performs the prescribed action solely because it ought to be done, relinquishing attachment and also fruits, his relinquishment is deemed to be of the nature of goodness. (9)

He, who neither abhors unpleasant action nor delights in a pleasant one, such a relinquisher, absorbed in goodness, is wise and his doubts are dispelled. (10)

For it is truly impossible for an embodied being to relinquish actions entirely; but one who relinquishes the fruits of action is called a relinquisher. (11)

The triple fruits of action—good, harmful and mixed—haunt everyone after death who does not relinquish, but never a person of relinquishment. (12)

O mighty-armed (Arjuna), learn from me the five causes for the accomplishment of all actions as they have been explained in the *Samkhya*. (13)

They are the material basis, the agent, the manifold instrumentality (i.e., the senses), various divergent attempts and finally, the fifth of these, the divine plan. (14)

Whatever action one initiates through body, speech, and mind—either proper or improper, these are its five causes. (15)

This being so, when a man of false notions sees himself as the sole agent due to his poor understanding, he does not (really) see. (16)

One who is not egotistical, whose understanding is not tainted, even if he kills these people, he does not kill nor is he bound (by the killings). (17)

Knowledge, the object of knowledge and the knower constitute the triple stimulus of action; the instrument, the act and the agent are the threefold components of action. (18)

Knowledge, action and the agent are threefold too, differentiated by the *gunas* as declared in the theory of the *gunas*; hear of them also as they are. (19)

The knowledge by which one sees in all beings a single, indestructible existence, in the divided the undivided, know that knowledge to be of the nature of goodness. (20)

But that knowledge which perceives in all beings manifold entities of different varieties, different from one another—know that knowledge to be of the nature of passion. (21)

And the knowledge which clings to a single thing as if it were the whole, disregarding causes, without grasping the true nature of things, and is trivial—that knowledge is declared to be of the nature of dark inertia. (22)

That action, which is obligatory, free from attachment, which is performed without passion or hatred and by one who does not desire for any fruit of action, is said to be of the nature of goodness. (23)

But action that is performed by one seeking to satisfy desires, or again by one who is egotistical and acts with great effort, is declared to be of the nature of passion. (24)

Action undertaken due to delusion, without concern for consequences, loss or injury and one's own strength, is said to be defined by dark inertia. (25)

That agent is said to be of the nature of goodness who is free from attachment and presumptuousness, unaffected by failure or success, and endowed with resolve and enthusiasm. (26)

An agent, who is passionate, seeks to gain the fruit of action, greedy, violent in nature, impure, subject to easy excitement and grief, is proclaimed to be of the nature of passion. (27)

An agent who is undisciplined, unrefined, stubborn, fraudulent, malicious, slothful, depressed and procrastinating, is said to be of the nature of dark inertia. (28)

O Dhananjaya (Arjuna), listen as I explain (to you) separately and exhaustively, the threefold distinction of understanding and also of resolve according to the *gunas*. (29)

That understanding is of the nature of goodness, O son of Pritha, who knows (i.e., distinguishes between) action with desires and renunciation, dutiful and undutiful actions, fear and fearlessness, and bondage and salvation. (30)

O son of Pritha, that understanding is of the nature of passion which incorrectly understands *dharma* and *adharma*, and also what ought to be done and not to be done. (31)

O son of Pritha, that understanding is of the nature of dark inertia, which looks upon all things in perverse ways, is covered in darkness, and considers *adharma* to be the *dharma*. (32)

The resolve with which one sustains the acts of mind, breath, and senses by restraining their prostitution through the practice of *yoga*—that fortitude is of the nature of goodness, O son of Pritha. (33)

But, O Arjuna, the resolve with which one holds fast to *dharma*, desire, and wealth, with attachment, longing for their fruits—that resolve is of the nature of passion, O son of Pritha. (34)

The resolve by which a fool does not give up sleep, fear, grief, depression, and pride, O son of Pritha,—that resolve is of the nature of dark inertia. (35)

But, O bull of the Bharatas (Arjuna), now hear from me about threefold happiness. Where one comes to rejoice through long practice and attains the end of suffering, (36)

That happiness is called of the nature of goodness that seems like poison in the beginning but becomes like nectar in the end, being born from the clarity of self-understanding. (37)

The happiness that arises from the contact of the senses with their objects (and) seems like nectar in the beginning but like poison in the end—that happiness is recorded to be of the nature of passion. (38)

The happiness which deludes the self in the beginning as well as in the end arising from sleep, slothfulness and negligence—that happiness is declared to be of the nature of dark inertia. (39)

There is no creature either on earth or again among the gods in heaven who is free from these three *gunas*, born of Prakriti. (40)

O scorcher of foes (Arjuna), the duties of brahmins (members of the priest caste), kshatriyas (members of the warrior caste), vaishyas (members of the business caste), as also of sudras (members of the servant caste) are distinguished according to the *gunas* born of their own nature. (41)

Tranquility, self-control, austerity, purity, forgivingness, and uprightness, knowledge, judgment, and faith in the hereafter are the actions of brahmins, born of their own nature. (42)

Heroism, majesty, resolve, skillfulness, and also refusal to retreat in battle, charity and lordliness are the actions of kshatriyas, born of their own nature. (43)

Agriculture, herding cattle and trade are the actions of vaishyas intrinsic to their own nature; work that is essentially service to others is likewise the action of sudras, born of their own nature. (44)

Each one attains perfection by delighting in his own action; hear how one finds perfection by engaging in his own action. (45)

A man reaches perfection by worshipping with the performance of his own action the source of all activities of beings and by whom all this world is permeated. (46)

Better to perform one's own duty even imperfectly than to perform another man's duties well; performing actions determined by one's own nature, a man contracts no sin. (47)

O Son of Kunti (Arjuna), one should not abandon one's natural-born action even if it is flawed; for all undertakings are obscured by flaws, as fire by smoke. (48)

With the intellect detached from all objects, the self mastered, with longings gone, one comes through renunciation to the highest perfection of freedom from action. (49)

O Son of Kunti, learn from me only in brief how by attaining perfection one also attains *Brahman*, the highest culmination of knowledge. (50)

Being disciplined with purified intellect, and controlling the self with resolve, relinquishing sound and all other sense objects, and putting aside attraction and hatred; (51)

Observing solitude, eating lightly, restraining speech, body and mind; being ever absorbed in the *yoga* of meditation, finding refuge in dispassion; (52)

Freeing oneself from egotism, force, pride, desire, anger, and acquisitiveness; becoming unselfish and serene, one becomes fit to be one with *Brahman*. (53)

Becoming one with *Brahman*, becoming serene in oneself, neither lamenting nor craving, beholding equality towards all beings, one attains supreme devotion to me. (54)

Through devotion he comes to know me—what my measure is and who I am in reality; then knowing me in reality, he immediately enters into my presence. (55)

Even though continuing to perform all actions whatsoever, by taking refuge in me, he attains through my grace the eternal, unchanging place. (56)

Surrendering all action to me with your mind, make me your goal; taking refuge in the *yoga* of understanding, constantly focus your mind on me. (57)

If your mind is focused on me, you will overcome all obstacles by my grace; but if because of egotism you do not heed me, you will be destroyed. (58)

If clinging to your egotism, you think, "I shall not fight," that resolve is futile because (your own) nature will compel you to fight. (59)

You are bound by your own action, born of your nature, O son of Kunti; what you refuse to do because of delusion, you will be compelled to do even against your will. (60)

O Arjuna, the lord resides in the heart of every being; by his *maya* he causes all beings to revolve as if attached to a machine. (61)

O Bharata (Arjuna), take refuge in him alone with your entire being; by his grace you will obtain the eternal abode and supreme peace. (62)

This knowledge that I have taught you thus is more secret than any other mystery; after reflecting on it fully, act as you wish. (63)

Again listen to my profound words, the most secret of all; because you are very dear to me, I will tell you what is good for you. (64)

Focus your mind on me, become my devotee; offer sacrifices to me, bow to me; (and) to me alone you will come—truly I promise you—for you are dear to me. (65)

Relinquishing all *dharma*s, take refuge in me alone; do not grieve (for) I will free you from all evils. (66)

You must never speak of this truth to one who is without austerity or to one who is not a devotee; nor to one who does not care to hear, or to one who speaks ill of me. (67)

Whoever imparts this supreme secret to my devotees while giving me utmost devotion shall without doubt come to me. (68)

And there is no one among men who can perform more pleasing service to me than he; and nor shall there be another man on earth dearer to me than he is. (69)

He who studies this dialogue between us about *dharma* would be worshipping me by the sacrifice of knowledge—such is my conviction. (70)

If a man, with devotion and without finding fault, only listens to this, he too is freed and will attain the brilliant worlds of those whose actions are pure. (71)

O son of Pritha, have you listened to this with a concentrated mind? O Dhananjaya, has the delusion born of ignorance now been destroyed? (72)

Arjuna said:

O Unchanging One, my delusion is destroyed, I have regained memory (i.e. understanding) by your grace; with my doubts dispelled I stand firm, ready to act as you command. (73)

Sanjaya said:

Thus have I heard this wondrous dialogue between Vasudeva (Krishna) and son of Pritha—the man of great soul—causing my hair to stand on end! (74)

By the grace of Vyasa (epic poet), I was able to hear this supreme and secret *yoga* as declared by Krishna—the lord of *yoga*—himself in his very person. (75)

O King, remembering repeatedly this wondrous and holy dialogue between the Handsome-haired One (Krishna) and Arjuna, I rejoice again and again. (76)

And, O king, as I recall again and again that wondrous form of Hari (Krishna), great is my amazement, and I rejoice again and again. (77)

Where Krishna is the lord of *yoga*, and son of Pritha is the archer, there surely exist fortune, victory, prosperity, and sound morality, so I conclude. (78)

Philosopher's corner: Chapter analysis and questions for consideration

Krishna opens this chapter by revisiting the issue of comparative merit between renunciation of action and relinquishment of action. Renunciation is the abandonment of any action done with desire while relinquishment is the "surrendering of all fruits of action" (18.2). However, this distinction itself becomes somewhat insignificant since neither renunciation nor relinquishment could mean abandonment of action but only abandonment of attachments to actions. This is so not only because our very nature is to act and thus every being is compelled to act (18.11) but also because certain prescribed actions like "sacrifice, charity and austerity" should not be abandoned (18.3) as they "purify the wise" (18.5). In the course of this articulation he reiterates that one gets bound or imprisoned by actions only when they are performed with egotism (18.58) due to delusion (18.60). He also clarifies that attachment to *all* fruits of action—"good, harmful and mixed" (18.12)—should be relinquished. He restates that through perfection in *yoga* and renunciation one attains *Brahman* (18.50). Krishna thus concludes, even though a yogi continues to perform all required actions, by taking refuge in Krishna such a yogi attains the eternal, unchanging place, i.e., Krishna's abode, through Krishna's grace (18.56).

Since introducing the detailed analysis of the three *gunas* and how they determine human nature and behavioral and psychological dispositions in Chapter 14, Krishna has also articulated threefold divisions in a number of areas from food to faith that correspond to the prevalence of each of the *gunas*. He adds to that list in this chapter by delineating the difference between three kinds—namely, of the nature of goodness, passion, and dark inertia—of relinquishment, knowledge, action, agent, understanding, resolve, and happiness. The common theme is that when something is of the nature of goodness, then it represents a relinquishment of attachment and is performed because it has to be done; when something is of the nature of passion, then it is marked by an attachment to desired outcome and is performed for that reason; and when something is of the nature of dark inertia, then it is marked by a failure to "grasp the true nature of things" (18.22) and is performed out of delusion (18.7). However, Krishna's discussion on the nature of threefold happiness provides an interesting opportunity in cross-cultural philosophical comparison. He explains the happiness which is of the nature of goodness in terms of a happiness "that seems like poison in the beginning but becomes like nectar in the end, being born from the clarity of self-understanding" (18.37). Correspondingly, a happiness that is of the nature of passion is one that seems like nectar in the beginning but becomes like a poison in the end (18.38) and a happiness that is of the nature of dark inertia is one that deludes the self in the beginning as well as in the end (18.39).

The nature of happiness has been an important notion in the context of Western ethics. Take for example the moral theory of utilitarianism championed by John Stuart Mill in his famous work, *Utilitarianism*, where he argues that the moral worth of an action is determined by the "greatest happiness principle" which claims that an action that promotes the greatest amount of happiness for the greatest number of people should be considered moral. Most dominant versions of utilitarianism seem to share their understanding of the concept of happiness in purely psychological terms of feeling of pleasure and of aversion toward pain (see, for example, Mill 1979 (1861), 7). In comparison, the above characterization and gradation of happiness that the *Gita* offers provides us with a more nuanced ways of thinking about the nature of happiness. As an example of what Krishna might have in mind in relation to a happiness that is like poison in the beginning and like nectar in the end, we can think of an experience like going through the temporary pain and discomfort associated with knee surgery for the prospect of a pain-free knee later. I think the fact that this happiness should also be emanating from the "clarity of self-understanding" (18.37) gives us a hint that what Krishna has in mind here is more metaphysical and philosophical in nature rather than purely psychological. In articulating kinds of happiness in terms of what appears to be like poison or nectar at the beginning or at the end Krishna is not just focusing on psychological aspects of happiness. Something is like nectar or poison not just by being pleasing or painful to our senses but by being ultimately beneficial or injurious to us. Krishna thus extends the concept of happiness beyond its typical psychological confines.

In this regard one might propose that Mill's celebrated distinction between higher pleasures and lower pleasures is similar to the distinction Krishna has in mind here. In drawing this distinction between higher pleasures and lower pleasures Mill emphasizes the *quality* of pleasures in addition to the quantity in comparative analysis of pleasures. In relation to the quality Mill points out that pleasures whose appreciation requires the use of the higher faculties, the intellectual pleasure of reading poetry, for example, should be considered higher than mere sensuous pleasures. Mill's main argument in this regard is that those who are capable of appreciating both higher and lower pleasures "give a most marked preference to the manner of existence which employs their higher faculties" (Mill 1979 (1861), 9). Mill also clarifies if one is capable of pleasures involving the higher faculties then the likelihood of her being completely satisfied is far lower than if she were only capable of pleasures of the senses. As Mill concludes, "it is better to be a human being dissatisfied than a pig satisfied; better to be a Socrates dissatisfied than a fool satisfied. And if the fool, or the pig, are of a different opinion, it is because they only know their own side of the question. The other party to the comparison knows both sides" (Mill 1979 (1861), 10). The target of Mill's distinction is the hedonism of purely sensuous pleasures often associated with utilitarian views. We might wonder whether higher pleasure might be what Krishna calls the happiness of the nature of goodness and lower pleasures might be what Krishna calls that of the nature of passion. In Mill's higher pleasures intellectual and cognitive faculties that go beyond the senses are invoked as needing to be cultivated for the purpose of being able to appreciate the higher pleasures. However, while for Mill the focus seems to be on higher faculties, for Krishna the ultimate focus is on that happiness that is informed by an understanding of the true nature of the self. In this, Krishna might be giving us a way to think about happiness in non-psychological terms.

Another interesting idea that we have not encountered earlier in the *Gita* deals with the five causes that Krishna identifies for the success of all action. While he includes things like material basis, the agent, and manifold instrumentalities like the senses, what stands out in this list is the final item of "divine plan" (18.14). By including divine plan within the list of causes, is Krishna minimizing our ability to choose freely and thereby ultimately giving us a fatalistic world view? In the context of Krishna's main argument, divine plan makes sense since it argues that our ultimate freedom requires us to realize that we are not the agents we typically take ourselves to be but mere "instruments" of Krishna's grand plan. How these five causes of the *Gita* compare with Aristotle's analysis of four causes is another important location of cross-cultural comparison. In this regard verse 47 seems quite pertinent as well where Krishna counsels, "Better to perform one's own duty even imperfectly than to perform another man's duties well; performing actions determined by one's own nature, a man contracts no sin" (18.47). In fact this is almost a verbatim repeat of verse 3.35 which makes us think that Krishna might not want us to forget the idea contained in these two verses. But why is it better to devote oneself to performing one's own duties even if imperfectly? A simple causal analysis in terms of the fact that another person's duties are not within one's abilities doesn't work because Krishna in both these verses seem to be suggesting one might not only be able to do another person's duties but even do them well. So what does Krishna have in mind here? How are one's *own* as opposed to *another* person's duties determined? How does a person find these duties? As I mentioned in the Introduction, Aurobindo's essay titled "*Swabhava and Swadharma*" (1997) offers an interpretation according to which one's own duties (*svadharma*) refer to one's own unique path to and relationship with the Divine. Thus Aurobindo provides us a way to think about the above questions. Finally, while wrapping up this chapter when Krishna says, "If a man, with devotion and without finding fault, *only listens* to this, he too is freed and will attain the brilliant worlds of those whose actions are pure" (18.71, emphasis added), is he not undoing most of his counsel already? If the results can be achieved just from "listening" then why try to become a *yogi*? Or, could Krishna be talking about a different kind of listening here? If so, what might be the causal mechanism of such listening?

Selective Glossary of Sanskrit Terms

Adharma: Being the opposite of *dharma*, this stands for lack of or violation of duty; morality; law; justice.

Bharata: A descendant of the legendary king Bharata and belonging to his clan. This epithet's use to refer to Dhritarashtra as well as Arjuna in the *Gita* indicates that they belong to the same clan.

Brahman: The Infinite spirit; Ultimate reality; Eternal being; the Absolute. In some cases it is also used as a substitute for "Prakriti" (see 14.3, 14.4).

Dharma: Derived from the root "dhri" which means to uphold or sustain, this term stands for duty; law; morality; justice; moral merit. Among duties, it is used to refer to duties according to a caste; according to one's position within a family; according to one's particular station in life; The *Gita* also uses this term to refer to Hindu religion itself which encompasses all the above duties and law of morality (see 9.2, 9.3).

Guna: Qualities; properties; modes; psychological dispositions; moral attitudes; strands combining to form a rope. As Deutsch clarifies, "when the term *guna* is used in the *Gita* it is necessary to look closely at the context in which it is employed in order to see whether the physical, psychological or moral aspect is emphasized" (1968, 14). The *Gita* discusses three kinds of *Guna*s: *Sattva* or goodness, *Rajas* or passion, and *Tamas* or dark inertia.

Maya: Krishna's magic or power; Krishna's creative energy; cosmic illusion.

Prakriti: Primal material nature which contains all change and actions, actual and potential; unconsciousness material substratum; aspects of Krishna's nature.

Purusha: Primordial spirit of humans; Krishna.

Samkhya: One of the ancient philosophies of India which is later formalized by Isvarakrishna in *Samkhya-karika* as the classical Indian Philosophical school of Samkhya.

Veda(s): Derived from the root "vid" meaning to know, this term refers to the most authoritative among ancient Hindu scriptures consisting of Rig, Sama, Yajur, and Atharva.

Yoga: Derived from the roots "yuj," and/or "yujir" meaning to yoke, to control, or even to cease mental states, especially desires (Dasgupta 1975, 443). This term is used more than 150 times in the *Gita*. *Yoga* is used reflexively in the *Gita* to generally denote the act of yoking oneself to a particular effort to win a goal. The *Gita* distinguishes between three main *yoga*s, namely, knowledge (jnana), action (karma), and devotion (bhakti). Unlike the English term "discipline" a term most commonly used to translate *yoga* in the context of the *Gita, yoga* denotes a "broader concept." Further, "it is not the case that *yoga* has so many different 'meanings,' but that the central meaning is a complex one that in English is not exhausted by one equivalent. *Yoga* is always of somebody, in somebody, with something, for some purpose; *yoga* in an absolute sense hardly occurs in the *Gita* at all. When *yoga* occurs by itself it is oftentimes an abbreviation for *karma-* [action] or *bhakti-* [devotion] *yoga*. *Yoga*, then, implies (1) the process of a difficult effort; (2) a person committed to it; (3) the instrument he uses; (4) the course of action chosen; and (5) the prospect of a goal" (van Buitenen 1981, 17–18).

Yogi: A person who practices *yoga*.

References

Adidevananda S. (trans.) (2009) *Sri Ramanuja Gita Bhasya*, Madras: Sri Ramakrishna Math.

Ambedkar, B. R. (2002) "Krishna and His Gita," in V. Rodrigues (ed.), *The Essential Writings of B. R. Ambedkar*, 193–204, New Delhi: Oxford University Press.

Aurobindo, S. (1997) "Swabhava and Swadharma," in *Essays on The Gita*, 507–525, Pondicherry: Sri Aurobindo Ashram Publication Department (Originally published in 1928).

Bhandarkar Oriental Research Institute (1999) The *Mahābhārata* (electronic text) Pune, India http://bombay.indology.info/mahabharata/text/UD/MBh06.txt (accessed: September 26, 2017).

Bilimoria, P. (2004) "Perturbations of Desire: Emotions Disarming Morality in the 'Great Song' the *Mahabharata*," in R. C. Solomon (ed.), *Thinking about Feeling: Contemporary Philosophers on Emotions*, 214–230, New York: Oxford University Press.

Broadbeck, S. (2004) "Calling Krsna's Bluff: Non-Attached Action in the *Bhagavadgita*," *Journal of Indian Philosophy* 32: 81–103.

Chakrabarti, A. (1988) "The End of Life: A Nyaya-Kantian Approach to the *Bhagavadgita*," *Journal of Indian Philosophy* 16: 327–334.

Chidbhavananda, S. Swami (trans.) (1997) *The Bhagavad Gita*, Tirupparaitturai: Sri Ramkrishna Tapovanam.

Dasgupta, S. N. (1975) "The Philosophy of the *Bhagavad-Gita*," in *A History of Indian Philosophy* vol. II, 437–552, Delhi: Motilal Banarasidass (Originally published in 1922).

Deshpande, M. M. (1991) "The Epic Context of the *Bhagavadgita*," in A. Sharma (ed.), *Essays on the Mahabharata*, 334–348, Leiden: E. J. Brill.

Deutsch, E. (1968) *The Bhagavad Gita: Translated, with Introduction and Critical Essays*, New York: Holt, Rinehart and Winston.

Easwaran, E. (2007) *The Bhagavad Gita* (Introduced and translated), Canada: Nilgiri Press.

Edgerton, F. (trans.) (1972) *The Bhagavad Gita*, Cambridge, MA: Harvard University Press (Originally published in 1944).

Flood, G. and Martin C. (2012) *The Bhagavad Gita: A New Translation*, New York: W. W. Norton & Company.

Frankfurt, H. G. (1971) "Freedom of the Will and the Concept of a Person," *The Journal of Philosophy* 68 (1): 5–20.

Gandhi, M. (2009) *The Bhagavad Gita According to Gandhi: Text and Commentary Translated from Gujarati*, Berkeley, CA: North Atlantic Books.

Griffith, R. T. H. (trans.) (1896) *The Hymns of the Rigveda*, Benaras: E. J. Lazarus and Co..

Gupta, B. (2006) "*Bhagavad Gita* as Duty and Virtue Ethics," *Journal of Religious Ethics* 34 (3): 373–395.

Hutton, J. H. (1969) *Caste in India*, 4th edn, Bombay: Oxford University Press.

James, W. (1997) *The Varieties of Religious Experience: A Study in Human Nature*, New York: Simon & Schuster (Originally published in 1902).

Johnson, K. A. (2007) "The Social Construction of Emotions in the *Bhagavad Gita*," *Journal of Religious Ethics* 35 (4): 655–679.

Kunkel, J. (2006) "The Spiritual Side of Peacemaking," in D. Boersema & K. G. Brown (eds), *Spiritual and Political Dimensions of Nonviolence and Peace*, 31–41, Amsterdam: Rodopi.

Larson, G. J. (1981) "The Song Celestial: Two Centuries of the *Bhagavad Gita* in English," *Philosophy East and West* 31 (4): 513–541.

Larson, G. J. (2000) "Hinduism in India and in America," in J. Neusner (ed.), *World Religions in America: An Introduction*, 124–141, Louisville, KY: Westminster John Knox Press.

Maitra, K. (2006) "Comparing the *Bhagavad-Gita* and Kant: A Lesson in Comparative Philosophy," *Philosophy in the Contemporary World* 13 (1, Spring): 63–67.

Malhotra, A. K. (1999) *Transcreation of the* Bhagavad Gita, New Jersey: Prentice Hall.

Mani, L. (1989) "Contentious Traditions: The Debate on Sati in Colonial India," in K. Sangari & S. Vaid (eds), *Recasting Women: Essays in Colonial History*, 88–126, India: Kali for Women.

Marjanovic, B. (trans.) (2004) *Abhinavagupta's Commentary on the Bhagavad Gita*, Varanasi: Indica Books.

Mill, J. S. (1979) *Utilitarianism*, Indianapolis: Hackett Publishing Company (Originally published in 1861).

Miller, B. S. (trans.) (1986) *The Bhagavad-Gita: Krishna's Counsel in Time of War*, New York: Bantam Dell.

Minor, R. (1986) *Modern Indian Interpreters of the Bhagavad Gita*, Albany: SUNY Press.

Nadkarni, M. V. (2017) *The Bhagavad-Gita for the Modern Reader: History, Interpretations and Philosophy*, London: Routledge.

Patel, R. N. (1991) *Philosophy of the* Gita, New York: Peter Lang.

Perrett, R. W. (1998) *Hindu Ethics: A Philosophical Study*, Honolulu: University of Hawaii Press.

Phillips, S. H. (2009) *Yoga, Karma, and Rebirth: A Brief History and Philosophy*, New York: Columbia University Press.

Radhakrishnan, S. (1948) *The Bhagavadgita: With an Introductory Essay, Sanskrit Text, English Translation and Notes*, London: Allen and Unwin.

Radhakrishnan, S. & Moore, C. A. (1957) *A Source Book in Indian Philosophy*, New Jersey: Princeton University Press.

Robinson, C. A. (2006) *Interpretations of the* Bhagavad-Gita *and Images of the Hindu Tradition: The Song of the Lord*, London: Routledge.

Sharma, A. (1986) *The Hindu Gita: Ancient and Classical Interpretations of the Bhagavadgita*, La Salle: Open Court.

Sharpe, E. J. (1985) *The Universal Gita: Western Images of the Bhagavadgita*, London: Duckworth.

Teschner, G. (1992) "Anxiety, Anger and the Concept of Agency and Action in the Bhagavad Gita," *Asian Philosophy* 2 (1): 61–78.

Theodor, I. (2010) *Exploring the* Bhagavad Gita*: Philosophy, Structure and Meaning*, London: Ashgate.

van Buitenen, J. A. B. (1981) *The* Bhagavadgita *in the* Mahabharata*: Text and Translation*, Chicago: University of Chicago Press.

Zaehner, R. C. (1969) *The Bhagavad-Gita: With a Commentary Based on the Original Sources*, London: Oxford University Press.

Zelliot, E. (2001) *From Untouchability to Dalit: Essays on the Ambedkar Movement*, New Delhi: Manohar.

Index

Abhinavagupta, 27–8
aboutness, 81
Achyuta, 35
action
  abandon(ing) the fruit of
    action, 70
  abstaining from action/
    abstention from action, 54,
    57
  action in inaction, 63, 66
  actionlessness, 53, 54, 57
  bondage of action, 45
  born of action, 64
  bound by action, 54, 63
  dynamics between action and
    inaction, 67
  followers of action, 54
  fruits of action, 70, 76, 133,
    159, 160
  intentional action, 11, 57
  locus of all actions, 66
  mechanism of action, 58
  nature of action, 61
  non-attached action, 23, 26–7,
    32
  organs of action, 54
  perfection by action, 55
  perform(ing) action only with
    the body, 70
  physical action, 66
  prescribed action, 15, 26, 158,
    164
  selfless action, 53
  skill in actions, 46
  source of action, 53
  teleological view of action, 27
  threefold components of
    action, 159
  triple fruits of action, 158
  triple stimulus of action, 159
  way of action, 63
  without attachment, 55, 58–9,
    73, 100
  wrong action, 61, 63
adharma, 21, 36, 38, 62, 65, 160,
  169
Adidevananda, S, 130
adrishta, 11
agency, 24, 27, 32, 51, 59, 71,
  115, 126
  agency and individuality, 53
  false sense of agency, 58
  location of agency, 58, 128
  sense of agency, 32, 58, 72
  women's agency, 38
agent, 11, 17, 30, 55, 57, 58, 133,
  159, 160, 165, 167
  agent of confusion, 55
Agni, 31, 111
ahamkara/subjectification, 17
air, 83, 84, 97
allegorical, 66
all-pervading, 44, 114, 117, 118,
  126, 129
Ambedkar, B. R., 21, 22
ambidextrous archer, 111
anger, 25, 46, 47, 49, 56, 62, 71,
  72, 145, 146, 147, 149, 162
appearance and reality, 48
approach, 4–5

coherentist, 5
multitrack, 5
multitrack coherentism, 5
single-track approach, 5
argument by analogy, 129
Aristotelean theme of the golden
   mean, 81
Arjuna's dilemma, 9, 15–16, 37,
   48, 115
arrogance, 145, 146, 147, 148
Aryan, 12
ascetics, 64, 72, 84, 91
ashvattha, 104, 105, 139, 140,
   141–2
Ashvatthama, 34
Asita, 102
atheistic, 128
atman, 27
attachment
   abandoning/having abandoned
      attachment, 25, 46, 64, 70
   attachment to action, 132, 164
   attachment to the fruits of
      action, 27, 164
   attachment to happiness, 132,
      135
   attachment to outcome, 41
   attachment to the world, 50
   free(d) from attachment, 113,
      119, 159
   non-attachment, 28, 78, 81, 87,
      93, 129, 139, 140
   without attachment, 27, 50,
      53, 54, 55, 58, 59, 61, 72,
      73, 100
attraction, 47, 56, 162
attributes, 124
Aurobindo, Sri, 13, 31, 167
austerity/austerities, 31, 64, 72,
   79, 84, 92, 98, 102, 112,
   113, 115, 146, 151, 152, 153,
   154, 155, 158, 161, 163, 164
   austerity of knowledge, 62
avatar, 66

Bādarāyaṇa, 130
Being of Boundless Form, 111
beginningless, 102, 123, 125,
   126
best of the Bharatas, 152, 158
best of the embodied ones, 90
best of Gods, 110
best of the Kurus, 64, 103
best of men, 43
best of the Purushas, 90
Bhakti, 22, 23, 30, 60, 170
Bharata, 8, 35, 43, 44, 55, 62, 65,
   86, 108, 124, 126, 132, 141,
   146, 162, 169
   bull of the Bharatas, 57, 85,
      92, 126, 133, 152, 160
Bhima, 34, 39
Bhishma/Devavrata/grand sire, 8,
   9, 34, 35, 39, 42, 110, 111,
   115
"Bible" of Hinduism, 20
Bilimoria, Purushottama, 49
blameless one, 54
body, 10, 16, 19, 25, 26, 36, 43,
   44, 48, 54, 56, 62, 63, 69,
   70, 71, 73, 77, 79, 81, 90,
   91, 93, 108, 109, 112, 124,
   126, 129, 131, 132, 133,
   136, 140, 141, 152, 153,
   159, 162
   body's gates, 91
   psycho-physical body, 17
bondage, 17, 25, 26, 45, 56,
   66, 67, 129, 145, 146,
   149, 160
   freed from bondage, 70
Brahma, 31, 91, 109, 111, 130,
   142
   Brahma's cosmic realm, 91
   Brahma's night, 91
   day of Brahma/Brahma's day,
      91
Brahman, 6, 14–15, 16, 24, 28,
   30, 47, 55, 64, 67, 70, 71,

74, 78, 79, 86, 87, 89–93, 125, 126, 127, 128, 134, 135, 153, 162, 164, 169. *See also* supreme *Brahman*
all-pervading *Brahman*, 55, 71, 127
established in *Brahman*, 71
eternal *Brahman*, 64
eternal freedom from *Brahman*, 71–2
Great *Brahman*, 132
immutable *Brahman*, 114
one with *Brahman*, 71, 78, 162
Brahma-sutra, 130
Brahmin, 12, 13, 19, 34, 45, 74, 98, 153, 161
scholarly and humble Brahmin, 71
breath, 64, 70, 91, 160
breathing exercises, 64, 67
ingoing and outgoing breaths, 72
inward and outward breath, 64
life-breaths, 64
vital breath, 91, 141
British India, 22
Brodbeck, Simon, 19, 27, 31, 32
Buddhism, 7, 141
Buddhist, 22, 31, 65, 136
Buddhist idea of middle path, 81

caramasloka, 30
care ethics, 37–8
Carvaka, 148
caste, 12–14, 16, 21, 22, 23, 31, 34, 36, 38, 41, 44, 45, 50, 71, 98, 135, 153, 157, 161
categories, 17, 28, 115, 123, 127, 128
foundational ontological category, 139
causal sources, 124

cause(s), 7, 26, 27, 34, 38, 44, 48, 55, 89, 104, 111, 115, 126, 127, 129, 167
cause of embodiment, 133, 135
first cause, 111
five causes, 157, 159, 167
Chakrabarti, Arindam, 26
chariot-warriors, 34, 45
charity, 92, 102, 106, 112, 113, 115, 146, 148, 151, 153–4, 155, 158, 161, 165
Chekitana, 34
Chidbhavananda, 39, 59
Christianity, 6, 99, 114
Christian mystics, 120
Judeo-Christian, 11, 99
citta-vritti-nirodha, 82
city of nine gates, 70
class, 7, 12–14, 16, 23, 63, 135
inter mixture of class, 14, 21, 36, 38
cloth, 77
coherentist approach, 5
colonial, 21
comparative, 67, 121, 149, 155, 164, 166
comparative philosophy, 23, 37, 50, 99
compassion, 102, 108, 118, 120, 146, 147, 148
conqueror of sleep, 43
consciousness, 16, 48, 89, 103, 118, 125, 128
dual consciousness, 28
moral consciousness, 17
pure consciousness, 14
consequentialist, 33, 41
contacts, 43, 49, 78, 140
born of contacts, 71
contact of senses with their objects, 43, 49, 161
external contacts, 71, 72
severance of contact, 78

content, 4, 46, 49, 63, 67, 76, 81,
  93, 102, 119, 120
contentment, 30, 55, 58, 71, 73
cosmic, 16, 89, 91, 140, 169
  cosmic form, 107, 109, 113,
  115
  cosmic perception, 114
  cosmic vision, 114
courage, 81, 104
cow(s), 54, 59, 71, 74, 104
craving, 77, 162
creative power, 89, 90
creatures, 47, 55, 56, 71, 72, 74,
  78, 99, 100, 102, 104, 111,
  117
  abiding in all creatures, 78,
  80
cross-cultural philosophical
  comparison, 165, 167
cross-species continuity, 82
crowned one, 111
cyclical, 11

Dalit, 21
Daoist, 67
dark inertia, 17–20, 85, 131–7,
  151, 152, 153, 154, 157,
  158, 159, 160, 161, 165,
  169
Dasgupta, S N., 5, 14, 20, 23, 30,
  31, 170
death, 18, 19, 28, 41, 44, 45, 86,
  87, 93, 95, 96, 97, 104, 111,
  115, 125, 126, 129, 133,
  146, 154, 158
  god of death, 101, 104, 111
  recurring deaths, 117, 118
  time/hour of death, 19, 47, 86,
  89, 90–1, 93, 136
deerskin, 77
deity, 85
deluded, 12, 55, 56, 58, 71, 72,
  79, 85, 86, 87, 92, 133, 140,
  147, 153

delusion, 47, 56, 64, 84, 86, 108,
  133, 136, 140, 141, 142,
  146, 147, 157, 158, 159, 162,
  163, 164, 165
  thicket of delusion, 46
demigods, 103, 107, 110, 152
demonic, 12, 85, 97, 145–9, 152
demon(s), 35, 103, 104, 105, 107,
  110, 111, 152
Deshpande, Madhav M., 4, 31
desire, 6, 12, 25, 26, 36, 46, 47,
  49, 54, 56, 57, 58, 59, 61,
  63, 70, 71, 72, 77, 78, 81,
  85, 86, 87, 97, 107, 108, 114,
  119, 125, 128, 132, 136,
  140, 145, 146, 147, 148,
  152, 158, 159, 160, 162,
  164, 170
  first-order desires, 136–7
  relinquished/renounced all
  desires, 47
  relinquishment of desire, 53
  satisfaction and frustration of
  desires, 73
  second-order desires, 136–7
determinism, 19, 20, 27, 32
  fatalistic determinism, 115
Deutsch, Eliot, 4, 13, 17, 18, 19,
  23, 25, 29, 66, 169
Devala, 102
devotion, 15, 19, 23, 28–30, 50,
  60, 67, 85, 91, 92, 95, 96,
  97, 98, 100, 113, 115, 116,
  117–21, 134, 135, 157, 162,
  163, 167, 170. *See also*
  yoga of devotion
  person of devotion, 100
  undeviating devotion, 132
  unwavering devotion, 108, 113,
  115, 125, 129
Dhananjaya, 25, 35, 46, 65, 84,
  96, 104, 109, 118, 160, 163
dharma, 7, 12, 14, 16, 28, 30, 32,
  36, 38, 44, 45, 50, 62, 85,

87, 96, 97, 98, 132, 160, 163, 169. *See also* duties
another's *dharma*, 19, 56
caste *dharma*, 36, 41, 50
conflicting *dharmas*, 43
eternal *dharma*, 14, 36, 109, 134
family *dharma*, 36, 37
field of *dharma*, 34, 38
multidimensional understanding of *dharma*, 50
one's own *dharma*, 19, 56
undying *dharma*, 119
Dhrishtadyumna, 35
Dhristaketu, 34
Dhritarashtra, 5, 9–10, 33, 34, 35, 36, 37, 42, 43, 109, 110, 169
direct, 75, 114
direct access, 10
direct experience, 96, 100, 113, 114
directionality, 81
discernment, 58, 96
discipline, 77, 92, 93, 170
acting with discipline, 55
disciplined, 28, 46, 63, 70, 71, 73, 76, 77, 79, 85, 86, 87, 90, 91, 97, 98, 118, 162
discrimination, 24, 54
disposition, 17, 18–19, 31, 79, 93, 124, 129, 131, 132, 135, 155, 169
behavioral and psychological dispositions, 131, 164
divine, 8, 10, 12, 14, 28, 31, 34, 58, 62, 66, 83, 86, 89, 90, 97, 100, 101, 103, 108, 109, 113, 114, 115, 145–9, 167
divine eye, 107, 108, 114
divine inner eye, 10
divine manifestations, 101, 104, 105, 106
divine *maya*, 85

divine plan, 159, 167
divine Purusha, 90, 91
divine *yoga*, 95, 96, 108
human-divine relationship, 100
perception of the divine, 114
Dnyaneshwar, 22
dog, 71, 74
Drafting Committee of the Indian Constitution, 22
Drona, 9, 34, 35, 42, 115
Drupada, 34, 35
son of Drupada, 34
dualism, 15, 48, 58, 59, 92, 127, 128, 134, 135
body-self dualism, 48, 58
dualism of Prakriti and Purusha, 17, 27, 127, 128, 134
methodological dualism, 134
mind-body dualism, 48, 81, 128
dualities, 24, 45, 51, 63, 71, 86, 87
delusion of duality, 86
realm of dualities, 87
Duryodhana, 9, 34
duty/duties, 12, 13, 16, 24, 25, 50, 57, 66, 146, 155, 157, 161, 167, 169
in accordance with duty, 155
caste duties, 12–13, 16, 31
from duty, 26, 155
duty for duty's sake, 59, 153, 155
required/prescribed duties, 7, 54
dweller of this body, 16, 43. *See also* self
dweller in this body, 43, 44, 56. *See also* embodied self

earth, 17, 35, 41, 45, 56, 63, 83, 84, 107, 109, 141, 161, 163
Easwaran, Eknath, 38, 99, 120

Edgerton, Franklin, 4, 12, 14, 28, 30, 39
ego, 30, 84, 114, 139
egotism, 145–7, 152, 162, 164
elements, 15, 24, 105, 114, 121, 124, 127, 152
elephant, 71, 104
embodied, 30, 48, 58, 81, 132, 133
    embodied beings, 117, 118, 119, 158
    embodied self, 16, 17, 23, 44, 47, 48, 70, 132, 140, 152
embryo, 56, 132
empty, 81
enemy, 56, 57, 76, 147
engagement, 32, 38, 48, 50, 80, 113, 120, 124
    attitude of engagement, 80
    world-renouncing disengagement, 80
enlightenment, 32
envy, 63
epistemology, 49, 73, 123, 127
    virtue epistemology, 129
equal, 34, 112, 121, 134, 147, 149
    equal eye, 106, 120
    equal vision, 69
equality, 74, 162
equanimity, 24, 25, 42, 50, 51, 73, 74, 75, 80, 82, 87, 102, 106, 118, 120, 121, 131
    attitude of equanimity, 80
    cognitive dimension of equanimity, 73
    constant equanimity, 125, 129
    equanimity in its ethical dimension, 73
    nature of equanimity, 69
    social dimension of equanimity, 74
    virtue of equanimity, 73, 120, 124, 131

established, 45, 54, 63, 65, 70, 71, 77, 78, 85, 126, 133, 134. *See also* established in *yoga*
eternal, 10, 11, 14, 36, 41, 43, 44, 48, 58, 64, 71, 72, 91, 92, 98, 102, 109, 134, 140, 141, 162, 164, 169
    eternal seed of all beings, 84
ether, 126, 129
ethics, 16, 23–30, 37, 38, 72, 73, 81, 149
    care ethics, 37–8
    comparative ethics, 149
    ethics of action without attachment, 73
    rule-based ethics, 37
    virtue ethics, 24, 149
    Western deontological ethics, 23, 73
    Western ethics, 165
even, 23, 77
    even-minded, 43, 63, 118
    even-mindedness, 42, 120, 121
    even temperament, 75, 77, 81
everlasting, 44, 48
evil, 9, 30, 35, 45, 46, 77, 80, 126, 163
    destruction of the evil-doers, 62, 65
    evil-doer(s), 10, 62, 65
    freed from evil, 63, 96, 102
evolution, 20, 93, 127
    cosmic evolution, 16
    evolutes, 127
excessive pride, 146
exhalation, 64
experience, 6, 21, 42, 43, 47, 48, 49, 50, 56, 96, 99, 100, 113, 114, 126, 128, 129, 134, 165
    religious experience, 114

faintheartedness, 42

faith, 29, 31, 79, 85, 96, 98, 117,
    118, 119, 151–5, 161, 164
    faithful, 65, 67, 79
    faithless, 65

fame, 44, 102, 104, 106

family, 4, 9, 10, 14, 15, 36–7, 38,
    79, 115, 169
    destruction of family, 36, 38

fatalistic, 115, 167

father of atomic bomb, 113. *See
    also* Oppenheimer

fear, 45, 46, 49, 62, 72, 77, 112,
    119, 158, 160

feminine powers, 104, 105

field, 17, 34, 38, 108, 123–30
    field-knower, 123, 124, 126,
        127, 128
    field of Kuru, 38
    lord of the field, 126, 127

fiery hero, 105

fire, 22, 30, 44, 56, 63, 64, 67,
    76, 83, 84, 92, 97, 103, 109,
    111, 120, 140, 161
    fires of restraint, 64
    fires of the senses, 64
    fires of time, 110
    fire of *yoga*, 64
    insatiable fire, 56
    kindled fire, 64

firmness, 78

fixed, 44, 90, 118, 120

flawless, 71

foe(s), 42, 62, 64, 76, 77, 80, 96,
    119, 120, 134, 161

food, 23, 31, 42, 47, 54, 55, 64,
    67, 77, 80, 81, 141, 151,
    152, 154, 155, 164

forgiveness, 102, 104, 105, 112,
    146, 147

formalism, 59

fortitude, 104, 105, 160

four-armed form, 112

fourfold order, 63. *See also*
    "classes" and "caste"

Frankfurt, Harry, 136

free, 17, 30, 45, 46, 47, 58, 61,
    63, 70, 77, 84, 85, 113, 118,
    119, 125, 127, 159, 160,
    161, 163
    free from desire and anger, 72
    free from fear, 77, 112

freedom, 12, 17, 28, 32, 59, 90,
    93, 127, 146, 148, 157, 161,
    167
    eternal freedom, 69, 71, 72, 74
    freedom from old age and
        death, 86, 87
    spiritual freedom, 96
    supreme freedom, 77

friend(s), 35, 36, 38, 62, 76, 77,
    79, 80, 97, 99, 112, 119,
    120, 134
    friend of all beings, 72

fruit(s), 1, 25, 45, 46, 63, 70, 71,
    92, 98, 100, 133, 152, 153,
    158, 160
    fruit(s) of action, 7, 25, 27, 29,
        42, 46, 63, 70, 73, 76, 118,
        120, 133, 157, 158, 159,
        160, 164

fuel, 64

gain, 41, 42, 45, 55, 65, 78, 106,
    160

Gandhi, Mahatma, 1, 38

gaze, 72, 81, 110

Gita Bhasya, 130

goal(s), 2, 5, 19, 24, 26, 29, 30,
    31, 32, 45, 51, 57, 58, 73,
    80, 97, 99, 113, 118, 119,
    120, 125, 126, 136, 139,
    148, 157, 162, 170
    final goal, 15, 24, 71
    highest goal, 21, 28, 79, 90,
        91, 98, 99, 100, 146, 147
    ultimate goal, 6, 7, 12, 16, 134

goddesses, 6, 29, 95

gods, 6, 9, 12, 14, 17, 19, 28, 29,
    30, 31, 32, 35, 43, 54, 85,

95, 97, 98, 99, 100, 101,
102, 103, 104, 105, 107–16,
119, 120, 145, 146, 148,
152, 153, 161
creator god, 95, 99
God of gods, 103
Judeo-Christian God, 99
multitude of gods, 102
offering to the gods, 58, 63
personal god, 29, 100, 128
worshippers of gods, 64, 85
gold, 76, 134
good, 9, 11, 13, 19, 38, 46, 66,
74, 77, 79, 80, 98, 105, 126,
147, 163
highest good, 54, 69, 87
goodness, 18, 19, 20, 131, 137,
151, 152, 153, 154, 155,
158, 159, 160, 165, 166,
169
nature of goodness, 152, 153,
154, 157, 158, 159, 160,
165, 166
Govinda, 43
grace, 28, 101, 105, 112, 162, 163
divine grace, 28
Krishna's grace, 116, 157
pure grace, 73
great spirit, 91, 109, 110, 111, 112
great warrior, 41, 44
great-armed warrior, 47
greed, 37, 133, 136, 145, 147
grieve, 16, 30, 43, 44, 163
Gudakesha, 35
gunas, 17–20, 31, 45, 56, 57, 58,
63, 83, 85, 114, 124, 126,
127, 129, 131–7, 140, 142,
151, 157, 159, 160, 161,
164, 169
gunas of passion, 56
gunas of Prakriti, 54, 55, 56,
58, 129, 161

handsome-haired one, 36, 46, 54,
103, 111, 124, 164

happiness, 26, 65, 67, 71, 73,
102, 125, 128, 131, 132,
135, 147, 151, 152, 154, 157,
160, 161, 165, 166, 167
eternal happiness, 71
greatest happiness principle,
165
nature of happiness, 165
perfect happiness, 78
threefold happiness, 165
Hari, 109, 164
Hastinapur, 5, 8
hatred, 56, 86, 118, 125, 128,
159, 162
heaven, 6, 11–12, 17, 42, 44, 45,
97, 99, 104, 107, 109
way to heaven, 99
hell, 11, 12, 36, 37, 145, 147
threefold gate of hell, 147, 149
henotheism, 29, 32
highest sovereign form, 107, 109
Hindu, 2, 5, 7, 8, 10, 11, 12, 14,
15, 20, 21, 22, 29, 30, 31,
38, 59, 65, 89, 93, 95, 96,
100, 113, 119, 169
Hindu philosophy, 11, 72, 73,
92, 99, 100, 115, 127, 130,
136
Hindu polytheistic system, 100
non-Hindu religionists, 113
Hinduism, 5–8, 19, 20, 29, 141,
143
Brahmanical Hinduism, 7, 22
Hrishikesha, 35, 43, 111, 158
human form, 10, 65, 66, 97
gentle human form, 107, 113
Hutton, J. H., 12, 13
hypocrisy, 145, 146, 147, 148,
152, 153

ignorance, 24, 58, 61, 65, 71, 72,
125, 133, 146, 147, 148, 163
darkness born of ignorance,
102, 132
ignorant, 55, 58, 65, 142

Ikshvaku, 62
illumination, 18, 71, 133, 136
illusion, 66, 169
immanent nature, 101, 113
immeasurable, 43, 109, 111, 146
immortal, 16, 48, 103, 104, 134
immortality, 95, 97, 125, 133
   fit for immortality, 43
immovable, 44, 118, 142
immutable, 44, 48, 63, 86, 89,
      91, 108, 109, 114, 118, 134,
      141, 142
impartial(s), 25, 46, 77
impartiality, 25, 59, 67, 120, 121,
      155
imperative, 59
   categorical imperative, 59,
      121, 155
imperishable, 43, 55, 62, 91, 97,
      100, 109, 111, 117, 118, 119,
      120, 123, 126, 131, 133
inaction, 25, 61, 63, 66
   inaction in action, 63, 66, 67
incarnated, 61
incarnation, 7, 29, 65
independent, 8, 11, 17, 24, 27, 45,
      63, 115
indestructible, 41, 43, 44, 90, 97,
      104, 139, 141, 142, 159
Indian philosophy, 4, 37, 81–2,
      114, 129, 148, 169
individuality, 47, 53, 55, 58, 83, 84
Indra, 6, 12, 97, 103, 104. See
      also Vasava
I-ness, 118, 124, 125, 127
infamy, 102, 106
infinite, 16, 76, 77, 109, 111, 127,
      169
   infinite form, 107, 109, 115
inhalation, 64
inherent nature, 71, 89, 90
instrumentality, 114, 159
   instrumentality of pure ideas,
      114

intellect, 27, 42, 45, 46, 47, 49,
      50, 57, 69, 70, 72, 73, 77,
      78, 79, 83, 84, 124, 127,
      161, 162
   destruction of intellect, 47, 49
intent, 47, 70, 72, 119, 140
   willful intent, 78
intention(s), 26, 57, 67
intentional
   intentional action, 11, 57, 66
   intentional content, 49, 81
intentionality, 49, 80
irresolute men, 45
Islam, 6, 99
Isvarakrishna, 31, 127, 169

Jain, 31, 65
Jainism, 7
James, William, 114
Janaka, 55
Janamejaya, 5
Janardana, 36, 37, 54, 103, 113
Jayadratha, 111
jiva, 48
Johnson, Kathryn Ann, 49
joy, 6, 20, 36, 47, 50, 96, 118, 119,
      126, 134
   infinite joy, 76, 77, 78
   joy of the Kurus, 45, 79, 133
judgment, 84, 161
just war, 10

Kant, Immanuel, 26, 32, 59, 60,
      121, 155
Kantian, 23, 59, 67, 155
karma, 10–12, 15, 17, 18, 19, 20,
      22, 23, 26, 30, 50, 93, 115
   theory of karma/karma theory,
      20, 57, 66, 81, 136, 148,
      170
Karna, 34, 110, 111
Kashmiri Shaiva tradition, 27
Kaurava, 9, 10, 65
king of Kashi, 34, 35

knowledge, 6, 18, 23, 24–5, 28, 29, 30, 41–51, 53, 54, 56, 58, 62, 63, 64, 65, 67, 71, 72, 73, 75, 76, 79, 83, 84, 85, 86, 96, 97, 100, 102, 104, 105, 109, 118, 120, 123, 124, 125, 127, 129, 131, 132, 133, 135, 140, 141, 146, 155, 159, 161, 162, 163, 165, 170. *See also* sacrifice of knowledge; *yoga* of knowledge
    boat of knowledge, 64
    content of knowledge, 67
    fire of knowledge, 63, 64, 67
    imperfect knowledge, 56
    knowledge of the self, 67, 71, 72, 74, 125
    knowledge seeker, 85
    liberatory knowledge, 92, 129
    luminous lamp of knowledge, 102
    manner of knowing, 67
    perfect knowledge, 56
    theoretical and practical knowledge, 57
    true knowledge, 25, 30, 124
    virtue of knowledge, 73
Kripa, 34
Krishna
    Krishna as the abode of the universe, 110
    Krishna as the being with unparalleled power, 107–8, 112
    Krishna as the seed-giving father, 132, 134
    Krishna's agency, 115–16
    Krishna's counsel, 16, 42, 49, 50, 69, 73, 96, 167, 168
    Krishna's divine *yoga*, 95, 96, 108 (*see also maya*)
    Krishna's higher nature, 17, 84, 86, 97, 114, 134, 142

Krishna's lower nature, 14, 65, 66, 83, 84, 86, 89, 95, 114, 115, 128, 134
Krishna's supreme abode, 91, 93, 102, 111
Krishna's transcendent nature, 83, 85, 87, 89, 95, 101, 113 (*see also* transcendent self)
material and divine domains of Krishna's nature, 86, 89
Kunkel, Joseph, 82
Kuntibhoja, 34
Kurukshetra, 33. *See also* field of Kuru

Larson, Gerald James, 3–4, 5, 20
learning, 7, 82
    spiritual learning, 64
liberated, 7, 56, 98, 147
    liberated from the body, 71
liberating, 67, 92
liberation, 6, 7, 11, 15, 16, 23, 24, 63, 72, 89, 134, 135, 139, 145, 146, 151, 153, 157–68. *See also* moksa; salvation
longing(s), 46, 47, 56, 85, 133, 136, 160, 161
    freed from longing, 56
lord, 4, 66, 71, 97, 103, 109, 110
    great lord of the whole world, 72
    lord of all sacrifices, 98, 100
    lord of beings, 62, 97, 100, 103, 108, 111, 112, 126, 127, 128, 133, 140, 141, 147, 162
    lord of gods, 110, 111, 112
    lord of the earth, 35
    lord of the world, 71, 102
    lord of *yoga*, 109, 163, 164
    unborn lord, 102
lotus
    lotus leaf, 70
    lotus-petal-eyed one, 108
    lotus seat, 109

love, 58, 102, 104, 112, 120
   lord of love, 99

Madri, 9
Mahabharata, 3, 5, 7, 8–10, 19,
      31, 38, 39, 104
Mahar, 22
Maitra, Keya, 32, 60
Manhattan project, 113
manifest, 44, 85, 91, 93, 115
manifestation, 29, 85, 101–6, 113,
      120, 126
   divine supernal manifestation,
      103, 105, 106
   supernal manifestation, 102,
      103, 105
manliness, 84
Manu, 62
   four Manus, 102
materialist, 20. *See also* Carvaka
   materialist school of Indian
      philosophy, 148
Max Muller, 32
maxim, 59, 121
maya, 85, 95, 162, 169
   (Krishna's) own *maya*, 62, 65
   yoga of (Krishna's) *maya*, 86
medicinal herb, 95, 97
meditation, 50, 75–82, 118, 126
   constant meditation, 103
   meditation exercises, 82
   meditator, 81
   philosophy of meditation, 75
memory, 47, 65, 104, 105, 141,
      157, 163
mental, 18, 27, 30, 33, 49, 80, 81,
      93, 121, 135, 152, 153
   mental act, 66
   mental content, 49, 93
   mental realm, 80, 128
   mental state, 27, 49, 93, 170
merit(s), 12, 72, 97, 99, 154, 164,
      169
Meru, 103

metaphysical, 10, 66, 72, 74, 92,
      166
   metaphysical concepts, 89
   metaphysical confusion, 67
   metaphysical necessity, 74
metaphysics, 2, 5, 16, 17–20, 27,
      49, 73, 83
mighty-armed, 35, 56, 57, 70, 78,
      79, 84, 102, 110, 132, 158,
      159
Mill, John Start, 165–7
   Mill's distinction between
      higher and lower pleasures,
      166–7
Miller, Barbara Stoller, 2, 3
mind, 2, 4, 9, 18, 20, 23, 28, 30,
      36, 37, 42, 43, 45, 46, 47,
      48, 49, 50, 53, 54, 55, 56,
      57, 58, 63, 65, 66, 69, 70,
      71, 72, 73, 75, 77, 78, 79,
      80–1, 82, 83, 84, 86, 87, 89,
      90, 91, 93, 97, 98, 102, 103,
      112, 113, 118, 119, 120, 124,
      125, 128, 129, 137, 140,
      153, 159, 160, 162, 163,
      165, 166, 167
   embodied nature of the mind,
      81
   fickle and unsteady mind, 78
   single-minded, 100, 125
   vacuous mind, 81
mindfulness, 136
Minor, Robert, 20
moderate, 23, 77
moderation, 75, 81, 149
modifications, 82, 102, 124, 125,
      126, 127, 128, 129
moksa, 16, 23
monism, 15, 29
   personalized monism, 15
monotheism, 15, 29
moon, 84, 103, 109, 111, 140
   fortnight of the moon, 92
moral, 8, 9, 10, 11, 14, 15, 17,
      18, 24, 30, 32, 37, 50, 69,

121, 129, 148, 149, 155, 165, 169
  comparative moral theory, 121
  moral confusion, 41
  moral deliberations, 50
  moral dilemma, 8, 49, 115
  moral potency, 115
  moral psychology, 49
morality, 24, 38, 49, 51, 121, 149, 164, 169
Morrison, Diana, 58, 99, 120
mortal(s), 12, 97, 99, 102, 108, 110
motive, 4, 59, 121. *See also* maxim
multitrack coherentism, 5
mystery, 163
  deepest mystery, 96, 100, 108
  royal mystery, 96

Nadkarni, M. V., 22
Nakula, 35
Narada, 102, 104
nationalists, 21
natural hierarchy, 135
nature
  higher nature, 17, 84, 86, 97, 114, 115, 134, 142 (*see also* Krishna's higher nature)
  lower nature, 14, 65, 66, 83, 84, 86, 89, 114, 115, 128, 134 (*see also* Krishna's lower nature)
nectar, 64, 104, 160, 161, 165, 166
  immortal nectar, 103
Neufeld, 20
neutrals, 77
non-doer, 62, 63
non-dualism, 15
non-dualistic, 5, 15
non-violence, 1, 82, 106, 129, 147
  philosophy of non-violence, 82
normal conditions, 73
Nyaya, 114

oblation, 6, 64, 97, 154
obscured, 56, 71, 72, 161
offering(s), 36, 58, 63, 64, 67, 97, 98, 100, 115, 120, 127, 152
  offering of devotion, 98, 100
  pure offering(s), 62, 67, 72
OM, 84, 91
omnipotent, 14
omniscient, 14
OM-TAT-SAT, 151, 153
one-pointed, 75, 77
ontology, 48, 49, 75, 123, 127, 128
  ontologically foundational, 83
Oppenheimer, 113. *See also* father of atomic bomb
orientalists, 21
outcaste, 12, 13, 71, 74, 123
outcome(s), 11, 16, 25, 26, 33, 41, 57, 70, 87, 115
  desired outcome, 42, 57, 67, 72, 165
ownership, 58

pain, 11, 42, 43, 45, 49, 50, 76, 78, 131, 140, 151, 152, 154, 165
pairs of opposites, 24, 51, 70
Panchajanya, 35
Pandava, 9, 34, 104
Pandu, 9, 34
  son of Pandu, 34, 35, 64, 76, 109, 113, 133, 146
pantheistic, 106
passing away, 102
passion, 17–20, 25, 46, 56, 62, 75, 78, 85, 131–7, 151, 152, 153, 154, 157, 158, 159, 160, 161, 165, 166, 167
Patel, Ramesh, N., 5, 10, 15, 31
peace, 9, 47, 50, 72, 73, 82, 110, 118, 146. *See also* supreme peace
  eternal peace, 98

lasting peace, 69, 70
 philosophy of peace, 82
perception, 114, 125, 153
 cosmic perception, 114
 direct perception, 114
 extrasensory perception, 114
perfection, 54, 55, 79, 84, 91,
  118, 132, 147, 161, 162
Perrett, Roy, 2
phenomenology, 49
Phillips, Stephen, 11, 14, 31, 32,
  50, 60, 82, 137
physical, 9, 11, 17, 24, 26, 38, 48,
  51, 66, 114, 169
 physical realm, 80, 128
Plato's *Republic*, 13
pleasures, 18, 36, 42, 46, 71,
  166-7
 higher pleasures, 166
 intellectual pleasure, 166
 lower pleasures, 166
 quality of pleasures, 166
 sensuous pleasures, 166
poison, 161, 165, 166
polytheism, 29
 social polytheism, 15, 29
polytheistic, 6, 100
possessiveness, 47, 56
praiseworthy lord, 112
Prajapati, 111
Prakriti, 14, 16, 17, 19, 27-8, 55,
  56, 57, 58, 59, 66, 67, 83,
  84, 86, 87, 90, 92, 96, 97,
  114, 123, 124, 126, 127-9,
  131, 132, 134, 135, 140,
  142, 151, 161. *See also*
  gunas; Krishna's lower
  nature
 eight-fold differentiation (of
  Prakriti), 84
primeval, 92, 109, 140
primordial, 44, 102, 153, 169
 primordial activity, 140
 primordial creator, 54
 primordial poet, 90

protection of the righteous, 62,
  65
psychological, 24, 49, 51, 164,
  165, 166, 169
psychology, 26, 27, 49
psycho-physical, 17, 26, 128
pure heart, 100
purifying, 62, 65
purpose, 4, 16, 20, 54, 55, 58,
  76, 129, 142, 145, 146, 154,
  166, 170
Purujit, 34
Purusha, 16-17, 27, 28, 89, 90, 92,
  102, 123, 124, 126, 127-9,
  134, 135, 139-43. *See also*
  supreme Purusha
 ancient Purusha, 111
  highest Purusha, 128, 139,
  141
 primeval Purusha, 109, 139
 supreme divine Purusha, 90,
  91
Purushottama, 31

quiet, 80, 81, 82, 119
quietude, 78

Radhakrishnan, S., 2, 6, 20
rain, 55, 97
Raja Ram Mohan Roy, 21
rajas, 18, 85, 169
Rama, 104
Ramanuja, 39, 130, 142
reason, 4, 9, 23, 25, 31, 36, 42,
  73, 90, 93, 119, 126, 154,
  169
rebirth, 6, 7, 10-12, 15, 26, 46,
  62, 65, 82, 91, 93, 96, 129,
  139, 148
 conquered rebirth, 71
 cycle of rebirth/rebirth cycle,
  11, 82, 90, 93, 99, 123,
  129, 134, 145, 147, 148,
  149, 157
recreation, 20, 77, 81

refuge, 46, 85, 97, 100, 110, 162
  taking refuge in (Krishna), 19,
    21, 30, 43, 62, 84, 85, 87,
    98, 100, 118, 120, 140, 162,
    163, 164
reincarnation, 7, 66
rejoice, 71, 111, 119, 147, 149,
  160
  rejoicing in the good of all
    creatures, 71, 74
release, 25, 45, 64
relinquishing, 63, 76, 120, 157,
  158, 162
relinquishment, 7, 54, 118, 158,
  164, 165
renounce, 7, 26, 27, 118, 147
renouncer, 29, 76
renunciation, 1, 7, 15, 25, 26, 29,
  30, 54, 70–4, 75, 76, 96,
  98, 146, 157–68
  constant renunciation, 70
  renunciation of action, 26,
    60–7, 69, 70, 164
resolve, 27, 37, 45, 79, 104, 110,
  146, 152, 157, 160, 161,
  162, 165
  firm resolve, 78, 86, 97
  right resolve, 98
Rg/Rig Veda, 6, 97, 169
righteous, 10, 54, 62, 65
Rigvedic, 12
rites, 30, 76, 79, 85, 98, 112, 115
  rites of Pindodaka, 36
ritual(s), 7, 12, 13, 22, 25, 26, 45,
  99, 104, 110, 152
  ritual fires, 76
Robinson, Catherine A., 8, 20

sacred, 21, 105, 141
  sacred chant, 97, 151
  sacred grass, 77
sacrifice, 6, 12, 28, 31, 53, 54–5,
  57, 58, 59, 61, 62, 63–4, 67,
  92, 97, 98, 100, 103, 112,
  113, 115, 146, 147, 149, 151,
  152, 153, 154, 155, 158,
  163. *See also* supreme
    sacrifice
  acts of sacrifice, 58, 59, 151,
    153, 158
  enjoyer of sacrifices, 72
  established in sacrifice, 55
  highest form of sacrifice, 67
  inner dimension of sacrifice, 58
  inner sacrifice, 67
  lord of all sacrifices, 98, 100
  nourished by sacrifice, 54
  remnants of sacrifice, 54
  sacrifice of knowledge, 62, 64,
    67, 97, 163
  sacrifice with material objects,
    64
sages, 104, 105, 132, 158
  great sages, 102, 103, 110
  royal sages, 62, 98
Sahadeva, 35
salvation, 16, 22, 28, 30, 160
samatvam, 82
same, 2, 8, 23, 25, 26, 29, 30, 32,
  47, 55, 59, 62, 67, 69, 71,
  74, 76, 78, 86, 89, 91, 93,
  98, 100, 106, 112, 117, 119,
  126, 134, 135, 136, 140, 169
sameness, 24, 73, 78, 80, 81, 87,
  93, 135
Samkhya, 15, 16, 17, 31, 45, 49,
  70, 92, 115, 126, 127, 128,
  136, 159, 169
Samkhya-Karika, 31, 127, 169
samsara, 11, 12
Sanjaya, 3, 6, 10, 33, 34, 35, 37,
  42, 43, 109, 111, 112, 164
Sankara, 4
sannyasa, 15, 25
sattva, 18, 85, 169
  sattvafication, 135
Satyaki, 35
sciences, 96
scorcher of enemies, 42, 43, 86,
  113

scorcher of foes, 62, 64, 97, 161
seer(s), 63, 71, 102, 109, 124
   seers of ultimate reality, 43
self, 6, 11, 12, 13, 14–15, 16, 17,
      20, 23, 24, 25, 28, 34, 43,
      44, 45, 46, 47, 48, 49, 50,
      53, 55, 56, 57, 58, 59, 62,
      63, 64, 65, 66, 67, 70, 71,
      72, 73, 75, 76, 77, 78, 79,
      80, 81, 85, 86, 89, 90, 96,
      98, 101, 103, 104, 108, 110,
      113, 114, 125, 126, 128,
      129, 131, 132, 135, 140,
      147, 148, 151, 153, 154,
      161, 162, 165, 167. *See also*
      embodied self; supreme
      self
   conquered self, 76
   great self, 85
   nature of self, 42, 58, 66, 67,
      74
   phenomenal self, 80
   purification of the self, 73, 77
   purified self, 70
     real self, 80
   self-centered self-absorption,
     58
   self-centeredness, 73
   self-control, 47, 53, 57, 64, 82,
     90, 119, 153, 161
   self-deluded hypocrite, 54, 57
   self-doubt, 65, 67
   self-knowledge, 65
   self-mastery, 79, 118
   self of all beings, 70
   self-purification, 70, 77
   self-realization, 6, 53, 58, 59
   self's enemy, 59, 76
   self's friend, 76
   self-understanding, 160, 165,
     166
   transcendent self, 76, 80
sense(s)
   conquered [the] senses, 70, 76

   controlling the senses, 23, 54,
     59, 72
   object of sense experience, 56
   sense domains, 124
   sense-objects, 47, 57, 58, 64,
     76, 125, 140, 162
   village of the senses, 78
   wandering senses, 47
serenity, 47, 49, 50, 53, 153
Shaibya, 34
Sharma, Arvind, 20
Sharpe, Eric, 2, 7, 8, 20
shraddha, 155
simpleton(s), 70, 72
sin(s), 12, 13, 24, 25, 36, 37, 44,
     54, 56, 63, 64, 71, 79, 85,
     86, 97, 161, 167
   food of sin, 54
   freed from all sins, 55
   sins destroyed by knowledge,
     24, 71
   tainted by sin, 70
sinful, 21, 55, 56, 57
   sinful of all sinners, 64, 67
   sinful wombs, 98
single-track approach, 5
sinless one, 132, 141
Slayer of Demon Keshi, 158
slayer of demon Madhu, 3, 36,
     42, 78, 90
slayer of the foes, 42
social philosophy, 135, 136
Socrates, 168
solstice
   summer solstice, 89
   winter solstice, 89
Soma, 141
   drinkers of the Soma, 12, 97
son of Kunti, 3, 12, 35, 43, 45, 47,
     54, 56, 71, 78, 84, 90, 92,
     96, 97, 98, 124, 126, 132,
     147, 161, 162
son of Pritha, 35, 42, 44, 45, 46,
     47, 55, 63, 64, 79, 84, 90,

91, 92, 97, 98, 103, 108, 109, 118, 146, 154, 158, 160, 163, 164
son of Somadatta, 34
son of Subhadra, 34, 35
sorrow(s), 6, 20, 33–9, 46, 47, 77, 102, 132, 151, 152
    sources of sorrow, 71
space, 84, 96, 107, 109
species continuity, 82
speech, 45, 103, 104, 105, 146, 153, 159, 162
stable, 47
standard, 55, 105, 147, 149
state of beyond return, 71
steadfast, 43, 46, 50, 134
steadfastness, 42, 49, 125, 154
Stoicism, 30, 74
submission, 64, 67
Sudra, 12–14, 19, 21, 22, 23, 31, 98, 100, 161
sun, 24, 62, 71, 84, 91, 92, 93, 103, 109, 110, 123, 126, 135, 140
    thousand suns, 109, 113
suprasectarian, 31
supreme, 7, 24, 71, 77, 90, 91, 93, 96, 101, 102, 108, 109, 111, 113, 118, 123, 126, 127, 139, 140, 157, 158, 162
    supreme among men, 108
    supreme Brahman, 101, 102, 125
    supreme faith, 117, 118, 119
    supreme goal, 113, 118, 119, 120, 126
    supreme lord, 108
    supreme peace, 65, 67, 162
    supreme perfection, 132
    supreme person, 103
    supreme Purusha, 92, 141, 142
    supreme sacrifice, 86, 90
    supreme secret, 62, 163

supreme self, 56, 86, 108, 123, 126, 127, 129, 139, 141, 142
supreme shelter, 109
surrender, 28, 36, 102, 113, 115, 119, 155
surrendering, 56, 158, 162, 164
svadharma, 31, 167
syncretist approach, 5
synthesis, 5, 26, 30, 100, 143, 157

Taj Mahal, 80
tamas, 17–20, 85, 169
tapas, 31
Teschner, George, 32
theism, 15
    god of theism, 99
theistic, 5
theology, 99
theoretical physicists, 113
thick-haired one, 103, 108
thousand-armed one, 112
tiger among men, 158
timeless, 28, 36, 44
tranquil, 47, 76, 77, 78
tranquility, 76, 102, 106, 110, 161
transcend, 80, 92, 99, 132, 133, 134, 135
transcendence, 24
transcendent, 76, 80, 84, 87, 89, 99, 106, 113
    transcendent nature, 83, 85, 89, 95, 101
transcending, 59, 63, 118, 133, 134, 135
transformation, 57, 124
    internal transformation, 74
transformative, 67
transient, 43, 50, 99
trans-morality, 24, 51
truth, 16, 18, 37, 42, 44, 45, 48, 49, 54, 56, 70, 102, 105, 141, 145, 146, 148, 163

unborn, 44, 62, 86, 102
unchangeable, 14, 27, 85
unchanging, 16, 27, 29, 58, 83, 85, 86, 96, 162, 164
    unchanging one, 163
understanding, 2, 4, 26, 45, 46, 48, 50, 54, 56, 58, 59, 66, 71, 81, 82, 87, 90, 99, 100, 102, 106, 117, 118, 119, 124, 141, 146, 157, 158, 159, 160, 163, 165, 166, 167
    threefold distinction of understanding, 160
undertaking, 2, 33, 38, 61, 63, 69, 119, 133, 134, 161
unfathomable one, 112
union, 15, 23, 28, 32, 100, 126, 128. See also yoga
unity of reality, 75
universal, 121
    universal form, 109, 112
    universal law, 111, 121
universalizability, 59, 155
unmanifest, 44, 85, 91, 93, 96, 117, 118, 120, 124
unreal, 41, 43, 48
unrighteous, 54
unshaken one, 112
unthinkable, 14, 44
untouchable, 22
Upanishad(s)/Upanishadic, 6, 7, 13, 14, 15, 16, 20, 25, 26, 29, 134
    Muṇḍaka Upaniṣad, 6
    Taittiriya Upanishad, 6
utilitarianism, 165
Uttamaujas, 34

Vaisya, 12–14, 21, 22, 98
Varieties of Religious Experience, 114
varnashrama dharma, 12
Varshneya, 21, 36, 56
Vasava, 103. See also Indra

Vasudeva, 85, 104, 163
    son of Vasudeva, 112
Vayu, 31, 111
Vedanta, 39, 130, 141, 142, 143
Vedas, 6, 12, 18, 31, 45, 46, 84, 92, 97, 100, 103, 112, 113, 115, 140, 141, 143, 153, 169
    threefold Vedas: Rig, Sama, Yajur, 97
Vedic, 6, 7, 29, 46, 50, 59, 79, 91, 99, 124, 140
    anti-Vedic, 148
    Vedic orthodoxy, 15
    Vedic ritualism, 7, 22, 26
Vikarna, 34
Virata, 34, 35
virtue, 9, 24, 42, 48, 49, 53, 73, 79, 92, 120, 129, 149
    virtue of equanimity, 73, 120, 124, 129, 131
Vishnu, 31, 65, 66, 103, 104, 110
Vivasvat, 62
vow of chastity, 77
Vyasa, 10, 102, 104, 163

war, 1, 8, 9, 13, 15, 33, 35, 37, 38, 41, 103, 111
    inner war, 38 (see also just war)
    morality of war, 38
water, 36, 44, 45, 47, 70, 83, 84, 98, 100, 103, 104, 110, 111
web of pearls, 84
welfare, 97
    welfare of all beings, 118
    welfare of the world, 55, 59
Western analytic tradition, 49
Western ethical, 23, 148
Western philosophy, 80, 81, 128, 154
wicked person, 28, 96, 98
wind, 44, 47, 78, 103, 104, 105, 109, 110, 111, 140
    windless place, 77, 80

wise, 16, 36, 43, 46, 55, 56, 63,
  64, 66, 71, 85, 99, 102,
  140, 153, 158, 164
wish-granting cow, 54, 104
witness, 33, 97, 113, 114, 124,
  126, 129
womb(s), 21, 84, 98, 126, 132,
  134, 136, 147, 149. *See also*
  sinful wombs
  deluded wombs, 133
  demonic wombs, 12, 147, 148
  great wombs, 132
women, 21–2, 36, 38, 59, 98, 100
  women's corruption, 36, 38
  the "women's question," 21
world(s) 7, 12, 14, 16, 17, 19, 20,
  24, 25, 27, 28, 29, 30, 43,
  46, 48, 50, 54, 55, 62, 63,
  64, 65, 66, 67, 71, 72, 74,
  79, 80, 81, 84, 86, 91, 93,
  97, 98, 99, 102, 103, 107,
  110, 111, 112, 117, 119,
  120, 123, 124, 125, 126,
  127, 132, 133, 135, 139,
  140, 141, 142, 145, 146,
  147, 148, 153, 154, 161,
  163, 167
  phenomenal world, 6, 24, 86,
  123, 124, 139, 141, 142,
  151
  three worlds, 36, 55, 109, 112,
  141
  welfare of the world, 55, 59
  world cycle(s), 11, 95, 96
wu wei, 67

Yadava, 112
Yama, 31, 101
yoga
  ancient *yoga*, 62
  ascended/ascending to *yoga*,
  75, 76

buddhi yoga, 32, 50
constant *yoga*, 97
disciplined in *yoga*, 63, 70, 77,
  85, 91, 118
established in *yoga*, 54, 65, 78
ethics of *yoga*, 24, 51
  perfection in *yoga*/perfect
  in *yoga*, 79, 118, 164
person of perfect *yoga*, 65
renounced by *yoga*, 65
unwavering *yoga*, 102, 118,
  120
yoga of action, 15, 22, 23, 24,
  25–8, 29, 32, 53–60, 61,
  67, 69, 70, 72, 73, 96, 100,
  126, 146
yoga of devotion, 28–30, 60,
  116, 117–21, 132, 134, 135
yoga of knowledge, 15, 24–5,
  41–51, 54, 67, 72, 83–7
yoga of meditation, 75–82,
  162
yoga of renunciation, 61–7,
  69–74, 98
yoga of understanding, 50,
  102, 162
Yoga school of Hindu/Indian
  philosophy, 136
Yoga-Sutra, 82
yogi, 19, 24, 29, 42, 64, 69, 70–1,
  75, 76, 77–8, 79, 80, 81,
  82, 87, 90, 91, 92, 93, 117,
  119, 120, 131, 135, 137,
  140, 164, 168, 170
  great yogi, 103
  highest yogi, 78
Yudhamanyu, 34
Yudhisthira, 9, 35
Yuyudhana, 34

Zaehner, R. C., 1, 2, 12
Zelliot, Eleanor, 22